SMALL CONGREGATIONS

SMALL CONGREGATIONS

New and Selected Poems

THYLIAS MOSS

THE ECCO PRESS

The following poems from *Rainbow Remnants in Rock Bottom Ghetto Sky* by Thylias Moss, copyright © 1991 by Thylias Moss, are reprinted by permission of Persea Books, Inc.: "All Is Not Lost When Dreams Are," "The Warmth of Hot Chocolate," "Poem for My Mothers and Other Makers of Asafetida," "The Linoleum Rhumba," "Birmingham Brown's Turn," "The Lynching," "Interpretation of a Poem by Frost," "The Nature of Morning," "*An Anointing*," "The Rapture of Dry Ice Burning Off Skin as the Moment of the Soul's Apotheosis," "Almost an Ode to the West Indian Manatee," "Miss Liberty Loses Pageant," "Green Light and Gamma Ways," "What Hung Above Our Heads Like Truce" (revised and retitled "One-eyed Mother, Selling Mangoes"), "Congregations" (revised and retitled "Small Congregations"), and "Detour: The Death of Agnes" (revised and retitled: "The Wonder"). All inquiries to anthologize, photocopy, quote or reprint these poems should be directed to Persea Books, Inc., 60 Madison Avenue, New York, NY 10010.

The Ecco Press
100 West Broad Street
Hopewell, NJ 08525
Published simultaneously in Canada by
Penguin Books Canada Ltd., Ontario
Printed in the United States of America
Designed by Richard Oriolo
FIRST EDITION

Library of Congress Cataloging-in-Publication Data

Moss, Thylias.
Small congregations: new and selected poems / Thylias Moss.
p. cm.—(The American poetry series) $22.95
I. Title. II. Series: American poetry series (Unnumbered)
[PS3563.08856S6 1993]
811'.54—dc20   92-45683 CIP
ISBN 0-88001-289-7

The text of this book is set in Bembo

for Lewis because this is everything

CONTENTS

ONE

TWO

THREE

SMALL CONGREGATIONS

ONE

WASHING BREAD

In the river a woman washes
big white slices of bread
like shirts.

When she wrings them
milky water runs from wrists to elbows
and she remembers the loaf bloating
with starvation.

When she lays the bread on nearby rocks
she is a nurse swabbing fever.
It dries and gets dirty again.
Her children eat
pieces of their crosses.

FULLNESS

One day your place in line will mean the
Eucharist has run out. All because you waited
your turn. Christ's body can be cut into only
so many pieces. One day Jesus will be eaten up.
The Last Supper won't be misnamed. One day the
father will place shavings of his own blessed fingers
on your tongue and you will get back in line for
more. You will not find yourself out of line again.
The bread will rise inside you. A loaf of tongue.
Pumpernickel liver. You will be the miracle.
You will feed yourself five thousand times.

ONE YEAR SONNY STABS HIMSELF

One year Sonny stabs himself
setting up the tree. Ever stubborn evergreen.
All eyes watching. All us standing
there like somebody said, "Behold."
Beside me is the mama with her arms
draped down the chest of the littlest
and another young un fierce inside her.
Quite a scene and all on account
of that star, five-spiked wonder, metal
I hammered out myself in school. Crude
and no symmetry, one of the points curled up
to a hook. A star faceted like the turtled
sound blotches of steel drums.
Sonny bleeds
all over the pine top
and hasn't said a word yet,
hasn't pulled the star out of his hand.
All eyes seeing beautiful Christmas
in all the ornaments we made from little
pieces of our best things every year.
The mama just has enough sequins from
the sea-foam prom dress to get through
five or six more seasons. Now Sonny
giving up his blood. We just assumed
it would be tetanus. I found the metal
on the street; it came from something
that had already failed.
"When I see Jesus . . ." Sonny says.
All eyes watching
the sun go down.

ALL IS NOT LOST WHEN DREAMS ARE

1.

The dreams float like votive lilies
then melt.

It is the way they sing
going down that I envy and to hear it

I could not rescue them. A dirge
reaches my ears like a corkscrew of smoke
and it sits behind my eyes like a piano roll.

Some say this is miracle water;
none say dreams made it so.

2.

Long ago a fish forgot what fins were good for
and flew out of the stream.
It was not dreaming;
it had no ambition but confusion.

In Nova Scotia it lies on ice in the sun
and its eye turns white and pops out like a pearl
when it's broiled.

The *Titanic* is the one that got away.

FISHER STREET

I like to walk down Fisher Street.
Everybody hangs laundry in the backyard,

most of it white and durable.

I think of hundreds of gallons of bleach,
zinc tubs, clothes stirred with sticks,

Fels Naphtha, water hot enough to dissolve skin,

mortuary stillness forced on children during a sermon,
clerical collars stiff and sturdy as blades; this one

is a rude white, too much contrast with his face. I look away,

think of monks mashing grapes,
staining their feet the blue-black of a man from Niger.

I think they'll never get their feet clean. I see

Chix diapers white as glory; in heaven
they don't pee or shit

and it's a shame, the dead man's clothes
hanging dry next to them,

pants pockets pulled out and exposed,

shirts buttoned to the throat, sleeves at the wrist,
all faded, white after so many washings, all victims,
the widow's hair; everything

plain as day.

Songs rise in vapor, white and bleached
like all that laundry struggling on the line
like all of us
to be free.
I don't expect to see

any other angels.

WATER ROAD

Sing a song of commerce
for the long, long ride

setting out from Dahomey
and smelling well the first day

the sea, sea, sea I love
and tracing with my finger

fine outline of grayish bird
now diving, now rising from the water

a fist of feathers and beak
to shackle a fish doing the shimmy-shimmy.

Crew says: If it wasn't lovely, it'd be cruel.
Cargo says: If it wasn't cruel, it'd be lovely.

Then I smell too much us
and am close as love on two sides of me

but feel none. My finger still traces
but bird flies too far to sea's big

and it look for the water bottom to rest
but there be no end, no bed, no death,

no world like used to be.
We be deep in the ship, buried alive

in the tight, hot, sick world.
We be deep and floating on overflowing sickness.

We be men knowing down best.
We be women on the quarter deck

knowing crew men know down best
when they ram it down our throats

'stead of 'tween the legs.

Our eyes be like stars
be bright, be looking, be helpless

and hanging in black sickness
deep above.

ONE-EYED MOTHER SELLING MANGOES

What hung above our heads like truce
was also sky we think we cannot touch but
with eyes, horizons stay put like sadnesses.

What we would not even pray for in the alcove
our hands make, was already true:
Even the one-eyed mother selling mangoes
in the street makes sure her child looks great,

the white flounce collar peeled away from her throat
like the white fish flesh filleted by cool hands whose
long fingers forecast nimbus.

Her child is off to school wearing plaid
that looks so smart it need not go to school.

Here comes in the evening a breeze so narrow
it is an alley. Sometimes mangoes aren't ripe
and some fall off the tree and rot away and
there is no juice to celebrate.

If there be no mangoes next year, one-eyed mother
says, *we'll take this fine beach meal that our feet*
make finer, and fry a great big fish and make
a great big living.

One-eyed mother is so confident she finishes
a tea biscuit, the stardust falling from her lips
onto flounder scales
already aware of the weight of heaven.

THE BLUE TERRITORY OF
SISSIES

The sky's wild secret
is behind a blue as fixed and stable
as judgment just to look at it

but the sky is not even solid,
is just air made visible in light,
scattering like bugs in light's

sudden intrusion. Hysterical air
is all around. It can't stop.
It knows it is spinning though

it looks still to everything below.
The wildness that is frenzy that is
not adventure. That goes no further

than gravity. To crave it is
not to want much, and to be a fan of
the nervous breakdown that will not

fall apart alone, so the breaking out
of twisters, breaking up of houses
and towns.

At night the sky is not limited
to kindergarten exile above
a blue line. Exile resumes

when day breaks the dream. Darkness
only seems continuous and too soft
to crack. Then

in the lake's silver underneath,
the sky can see itself
holding trout and walleye.

It can see men walking into it
with cords and lines so kin
to what the lion tamer cracks

and doing so curls manes.
Despite this fish grab and suck
the lozenges at line ends as if

the men were fish doctors.
The sky can see this yet not feel
its skin ripping, its blue draining,

its soul ascending into the black
beyond and crashing into stars, a game
of pinball.

A jet stream surely is the purest
flowing yet isn't the bluest. And
for all that turbulent posturing

it would take much more than a sky
has done to shake the planes
out of it; it would take rebellion.

Sometimes it is as necessary as it is easy
to forget there is such a thing
as blue alert, issued

when it hasn't happened yet but
likely will, an air attack, some
unseen pushing escorting

the seventh wife of Bluebeard into
the forbidden room, turning Chicken
Little into barnyard Nostradamus

while the kites and flags flutter,
while in Kittyhawk
Orville and Wilbur sing unexceptionally.

GOSSAMER AND THINNER

The breast milk is so thin
it turns gossamer and a dragonfly

flies away with it all.

Thin like always
on the verge of running out, always
the glorious last drop.

Cows and goats
don't cry as much.

Flies away with it all.

Breast milk be pulled from me in ribbons
and baby be wrapped up in this and it's

hallelujah for the gift
and even hallelujah wears thin

if it's hallelujah this and that and
everything don't need to be praised,

everything don't need no deep search
for good, and some of it pulls more than

milk from the breast, the last drop
of hospitality, the thin wires of nerves

and that's a good boy and daddy's little man
and something going on is thin, cold and

Python can love a man to death.
I can't do that to a baby.

GAMES

Aunt Donna's Dead.
　　　—How'd she die?
　　　—Oh she died like this.
　　　　　　　(the child assumes either a grotesque
　　　　　　　or suggestive pose which the other
　　　　　　　players imitate repeating:)

—Oh she died like this.

—Uh-uh; Mookie shot her.
—That ain't how the game goes.
—I know it. Mookie shot her for real.
—Then Mookie's an asshole.
—Kids don't talk like that; you gon' have
to wash your mouth out with soap.
—You better get real.
—I did. And I don't like it.

Little Sally Walker sitting in a saucer—

　　　—Excuse me, but did you say in a saucer?
well; she can't hardly be black if she can
squeeze her ass into a saucer.
—Amen. Give me five!
—You think five saucers is enough for a black ass?
—You surely some self-deprecating nigger bitches!
—Who learned you to talk like that?
—I can't answer that. There just wasn't
anything else I could say
under the circumstances.
—There not supposed to be anything to say
under the covers.

—Yeah; you have to do the best you can
when you sleep. Aunt Besseth tell me
people who snore are so afraid of dying
they trying to wake themselves up.

Weeping and crying for someone to love her.
Rise, Sally, rise; wipe your weeping eyes;
put your hands on your hips and let your backbone slip.

—No problem. Right on your porch
then I'll call my lawyer and sue you; got
his 800 number right here.
—800 number? That's a hundred better than
The 700 Club.
—You know it! Girlfriend; you better repledge
your allegiance.

Aw shake it to the east,
Aw shake it to the west,
Aw shake it to the very one that you love the best.

—And, Baby, tonight that's you.
50 bucks please.
—Girl; you too cheap.
—We just playing.
—Yeah; well, it's still better safe than sorry.
—You mean safe sex?
—You can still be sorry about sex even if it's safe.
—Yeah; if it's not good.
—You're not a good girl.
—I know it. And I told my mother a thousand times
how sorry I am.
—What she say?
—She agreed a thousand times that I'm pitiful.
—She was probably just playing.

Here come Mrs. Sunshine
twisting down the street.
If she wants a husband, this is what she does:
Take some salt and pepper, sprinkle it on his toes.
Now go'on Girl, shake that thing.
Go'on Girl, shake that thing.
Back to back, Sunshine.
Side to side, Sunshine.
Face to face, Sunshine.
Now kiss him on the cheek.

  —Girls will be girls.
  —Boys will be men.
  —Boys will cheat.

MAUDELL'S MOON

Moon on your back, where you get
that moon on your back?

She stops. She just stands
and don't pose. She don't know
how she got that moon on her back.
She did not know she got the moon
on her back. She turn around,
she don't see no moon on her back.
    You lyin'.

Moon back on your back how you get
that moon back on your back?

    You got a parsnip? I'll trade you
    that moon for a parsnip.

Deal.

She walk on. She ain't had no moon
at all, but she got something now.

LIVING UNDER A MAN ON THE MOON

This is how it goes: They can put a man
on the moon even if they can't do
anything else. She is trying

to be grateful, so it's true
that anything is possible now.

She better get out there and get them
while they're hot, they're cooking,
they're whistling Dixie; while
they got the messianic method down cold.

They can put a man on the moon; she kicks
up her heels then sets her heels back on ground
less impressive, that someone else put man on.

Nothing is the same. She may as well dust
with her blouse and not think about how
it was assembled in Haiti when the sun was long gone
and moonlight provided what it could
with a man on it, watching.

She may as well let the white noise of the French
help her with duty. She may as well celebrate

while a Haitian girl attaches sleeves
and sees the moon through one of them when she dozes.
Don't wake her up; Haitian girl doesn't know them
or what they can do. It might come as a shock that

they can put a man a lot like the man on the stamp,
on the money, on the map, on bass, on first, on dope,

on her nerves; they can put just another man on the moon
that doesn't deserve this, the moon that has been faithful
as a dog, obedient to the leash of gravity; that lets
the man on it be ten times stronger, be the Hercules
that never was; they put a man on the moon and
everybody but her and the Haitian girl acts a fool
and thinks man now has new power; she knows
that putting a man on something as easy as the moon,
as cheesy as the moon, as vulnerable as the moon,
as promiscuous as the moon binging buxom, then
purging coy, then plumping for lack of protection
is nothing to brag about and does not mean talent
or genius; they put a man in a rocket
and he blasted off and landed on a virgin dead
world with a lot of craters that he just took
to be openings for his ego, his advancement.

She won't make love to a man that plays pool,
the cue stick a rocket to a ball of white opportunity.

THE WARMTH OF HOT
CHOCOLATE

Somebody told me I didn't exist even though he was looking dead at me. He said that since I defied logic, I wasn't real for reality is one of logic's definitions. He said I was a contradiction in terms, that one side of me cancelled out the other side leaving nothing. His shaking knees were like polite maracas in the small clicking they made. His moustache seemed a misplaced smile. My compliments did not deter him from insisting he conversed with an empty space since there was no such thing as an angel who doesn't believe in God. I showed him where my wings had been recently trimmed. Everybody thinks they grow out of the back, some people even assume shoulder blades are all that man has left of past glory, but my wings actually grow from my scalp, a heavy hair that stiffens for flight by the release of chemical secretions activated whenever I jump off a bridge. Many angels are discovered when people trying to commit suicide ride and tame the air. I was just such an accident. We're simply a different species, not intrinsically holy, just intrinsically airborne. Demons have practical reasons for not flying; it's too hot in their home base to endure all the hair; besides, the heat makes the chemicals boil away so demons plummet when they jump and keep falling. Their home base isn't solid. Demons fall perpetually, deeper and deeper into evil until they reach a level where even to ascend is to fall.

I think God covets my wings. He forgot to create some for himself when he was forging himself out of pure thoughts rambling through the universe on the backs of neutrons. Pure thoughts were the original cowboys. I suggested to God that he jump off a bridge to activate the wings he was sure to have, you never forget yourself when you divvy up the booty, but he didn't have enough faith that his fall wouldn't be endless. I suggested that he did in fact create wings for himself but had forgotten; his first godly act had been performed a long time ago, after all.

I don't believe in him; he's just a comfortable acquaintance, a close associate with whom I can be myself. To believe in him would place him in the center of the universe when he's more secure in the fringes, the farthest corner so that he doesn't have to look over his shoulder to nab the backstabbers who want promotions but are tired of waiting for him to die and set in motion the natural evolution. God doesn't want to evolve. Has been against evolution from its creation. He doesn't figure many possibilities are open to him. I think he's wise to bide his time although he pales in the moonlight to just a glow, just the warmth of hot chocolate spreading through the body like a subcutaneous halo. But to trust him implicitly would be a mistake for he then would not have to maintain his worthiness to be God. Even the thinnest, flyweight modicum of doubt gives God the necessity to prove he's worthy of the implicit trust I can never give because I protect him from corruption, from the complacence that rises within him sometimes, a shadowy ever-descending brother.

THE ADVERSARY

I could understand God's keeping Satan
to himself; you don't share
your best thing, your private stock, personal
ego stroker but God let the devil loose,
he says. Satan didn't just make up his mind
to leave, disgusted by the chauvinism
among other things. Let him loose
then hunted him down and bid us praise
the staging. The devilish contract
gets Satan second-banana high and
dismissed by jungle terminology.
The Joe Johnson against the Great White Hope
of a God.

The problem: God's need for adversary,
worthy opponent, for just short of equal.
And that's Satan, the runner-up, sprinter
in the next lane who could have grabbed the gold
if he could have afforded its blinding him,
the one who almost had it all.
As for God, all glowing is vain.

Satan accepts the rest. What rains down,
the heavenly sewage and trash, the blame
for holy wars, rescue rages. For every drop of blood.
For whatever will not be blessed, the unchosen,
Uncola. Some choose for those who do not
a Second or Third World, Third Reich.

In heaven Satan was a minority in a neighborhood
where everyone else was saint. Crosses burned and
his car, house, clothes, wings; all

his possessions. And the burning and reburning
of memories establishes hell.

Poor Satan. His authority denied him
by a nose, a longer, pointier Caucasian nose.
Where's the gratitude for Satan who is there
for God no matter what; Satan

who is the original Uncle Tom.

A FORM OF DEICIDE

Between Elvis, God, and Santa Claus, some people
get everything they need. Many travel
the roads to Tupelo and Emmaus and on the way
find long lost cousins among the Samoyed, other
scriptures, sacred bounty of the tundra's lichens,
mosses, stunted shrubs, and perspective.

In my seventh summer, the box arrives from Sears
and holds no antidote for August, just
Barbie and Ken, icons I take out for secret
ceremonies in my room until an hour before
my mother comes home. Santa comes in December
to officially emancipate them. There's real
Christmas joy though *I ain't nothing but a hound dog.*

One day I am grown; God must give me up, publicly
walk the aisle and surrender me. He will
always be my Father, but another man will be
my husband and I will look at him in ways God
does not want to be seen, so is invisible
and tempts not. Ever the strong, silent type
He waits for a wave of guilt to solicit

from a child or two, a prayer, card, delay
of golf to detour into His temple home there
to chat politely for an hour, sing a hymn.
Confined to church, to cross

as to wheelchair, as to deathbed; friars
and nuns tend to Him between visits. Muscles

atrophied long ago, the spirit is residue
no matter that it is eternal.

Bless this food, this sneezer, I say the next day
in command, giving the orders.

RENEGADE ANGELS

Every night women in love gather outside the window and it is nothing special; coming out is what stars do, clouds, the sun when it builds up the nerve and then has to just blurt out. Their thoughts collect there, outside, the window of no value to them unless they marvel at coincidence; the window is just how I know it happens. I am not part of the circle although every game I played as a girl was round. By morning there is fruit on branches not meant to bear witness anymore, that birds avoid and that embarrasses me so I don't taste it; I don't find out if they're edible berries, and even if they were, I'd let them shrink and drop dried; I can't see myself snatching berries, especially not from a shrub so brambled, the branches look as if the feet of little birds tangled and broke off to appease beaks that had to get into those berries no matter what. This is the wrong thing to say because someone will start thinking that women in love set traps, bait bushes, trick birds, act out fables in which birds are made to always fly, to exhaust their wings, to be up soaring to death because they can't resort to landing. This is how the great hoverers are made. But women in love can do more than this, making is too traditionally and industrially valued to be a special accomplishment, a reason to gather when light isn't that good and there are no decent shadows, and the lit square and rectangular windows are irregular stars so big in their closeness they can't be wished on and personalized; stars are better the more distant they are so that to wish on them is to empower pinpricks. My eyes do not close without seeing what darkness holds, the letdown hair of women and welcome. And I remember where I was when I was fertilized, where as a zygote I was stamped with most destinies but Eagle Scout, where I was when I divided and doubled without taking up additional space for a long time, before testing the limits of the skin that did not fail and being delivered; with a woman, deep inside a woman, expanding a woman's body from the inside, depending on a woman, filling a woman. This is what I remember while I'm saying that other prayer and singing that song I took, as a girl, as jingle: all day, all night, the angels watching over me. Outside my window. In honor of them for forty years I bleed libation.

OLD MAIDS WEAVING BASKETS

I was with you when Valhermosa
was a river, when we held hands
to fight the current,
came ashore, couldn't let go,
huddled in the church–like
shadow of Edna's house
and weathervane. Valhermosa's
a creek now, an unjoined seam,
lovers reaching.

We met under this linden
the day Edna married her cousin,
honeymooned up north.
From her yard she could see
everything: two sets
of underwear on a limb.
You got here first, hid
behind branches, a bride
helped by veil. Bared breasts
filled your bowl of a lap.

Today's no different.
Deliberately I kept you waiting
till Edna left the window.
Despite rumors
we have those baskets,
a respectable business.
Your feet dangle, insect bites
on both ankles, while we plait
grasses, sapwood cuttings:
motions learned from breaking
blessed bread.

Later we collect berries
in the freshly made baskets,
eat from each other's hand,
tremble,
echoes fearing error.
You said a man
would leave you.

THE ECLIPSE AND THE
HOLY MAN

The many-paned window in a cold room
made me see the winding oak in sections.

One consists wholly of old fingers
whose sensing the weight of air inspires
attempts to grasp it.

One part's bend is analogous
to the holy man's shoulders. He rises
out of nowhere as he walks up the hill.
He is dressed like an eclipse, a revival
of light behind him.

Where the window ends, the oak becomes
blue plaster, impenetrable sky that injures
faith which is so light, so unable to do
battle. I worry about the birds and

the problems cracks in the plaster point to,
why birds of prey are not holy, why
congregations of pigeons are not sacred
or saved though they eat the holy man's bread,
why the sign of the cross is communication
the hearing ignore.

Then the holy man walks away.
The eclipse is total.
One cannot prove the sun exists.
I worry about the birds.

ALTERNATIVES FOR A CELIBATE DAUGHTER

1.

This man is going to die without telling me.
It will happen while I dream of tornadoes,
those frantic clouds swirling in search of mates.
I won't be caught without a man
to order my life like an alphabet:
Albert   Bernard   Clifford   Desmond   Eric   Father's
going to die but I'm afraid
to hold his hand. If I feel something
daughters shouldn't feel   I won't let go.

2.

I don't choose men wisely.
When all else failed I went to Father.
Now he ignores me. He will not answer.
I shake him and he hardens into slate,
cold, smooth. What can I do?
I'm a trained daughter
yet the wreath I carry
could double as a bride's bouquet.

3.

The dream, almost a year old.
In it, his name for me is a flower: Hyacinth,
a final pink breath.

THE OWL IN DAYTIME

No one knows where the undertaker lives.
It should be impossible not to know.
In this village we find the owl in daytime
just to call him an ugly bird.

At night we have other habits
so we spill our guts to the owl,
tell him the worst tales we can think of,
how natural orifices evolved from wounds.
Yet the owl is too ugly to lose feathers.
Also, the owl has no neck.

Between the undertaker and the owl
there's no telling who's uglier.
Give us real differences, not night and day
that embrace each time they meet.
Give us the undertaker's daughter,
the bread she makes.

IT RIDES ON TADPOLES

I ate a little bread and felt better
walking the path so many have traveled,
no odyssey is left. I do not know

who baked it, the loaf rose around
a spring, so the spring in the loaf
must be the baker's signature.

As I walked I chanced upon the cistern
where people spit on others' wishes.

The saliva drifts
in bundles of bubbles which I fancied
under the influence of spring-cored bread
as tethered rafts of souls

whose former bodies have sunk fathoms
into deeper, wiser graves than earth's, below
man's capability of retrieval,
deeper than springs of want and need.

I imagined the bodies washed away cell by cell,
super slow-motion confetti, slow enough to fulfill
the purpose of anonymity: the reversal of fame,
restoration of the ability to fade so gradually
the exit doesn't finish and the scant presence
forms a light haze on asphalt, the ante meridiem
black ice spinning tires, seducing rubber.

I had stared too long at spit.

So long I could not spring back to my senses.
In fact, longing arrived, unkempt, tattered because
of who he is and what he must do. So it rides

on tadpoles that will drip out of a viscid mass
to proclaim spit and piss mysteries
unfolding, wonders of the world.

THE UNDERTAKER'S DAUGHTER
MAKES BREAD

Even a frigid wife yields, even a stud has a soft spot.
He's with one of them now, forgiving
any man who deserts a thoroughly paralyzed woman.
I don't forgive him

for making me believe in resurrections.
My belief is stronger than his or he'd work
in a tent and I'd be the faith healer's daughter,
myself cured.

Dough rises for me
no matter how I treat it, how I punch it.
Loaves line the counter like closed coffins.
Something I never want
is to wake from a long sleep
hungry.

THE UNDERTAKER'S DAUGHTER

FEELS NEGLECT

Tonight, a beautiful redhead
whose hair he's combed six times.
It is always the same. He never finds
his way to my room. My mother played dead
the night I was conceived.
Like him I'm attracted
to things that can't run away from me.
I spit-shine aluminum pans.

It's been years since the mailman came, years
since I woke in the middle of the night
thinking a party was going on downstairs,
thinking my father was a magician
and all those scantily clad women his assistants,
wondering why no one could hear me,
why I was made to disappear permanently in the box.
I seldom wake at all anymore.

PASSOVER POEM

God wipes his eyes.
God blinks as we do to resolve blur and disbelief.
He looks at the Jews he chose. They need a messiah.
He looks at my mother. Christ bought her with his blood.
Christ owns her. She is not free.
He looks at a million Latino boys called *Jesús*. Jesus.
And recognizes not one of them as his son.
He looks at Asian eyes and tries to steady his hands.
The bomb didn't do it all.
He looks at blood smeared on Sharon Tate's doors and walls.
"Safe," he says, more umpire than God.
Yet death does not pass over.
God blinks again. The earth is still there unchanged.
And poor God cannot pass the buck, he made the buck.

DOUBTS DURING CATASTROPHE

*The hand of the Lord was upon me, and set me down
in the midst of the valley; it was full of bones.*
—*Ezekiel 37:1*

Being in God's hand doesn't mean being in a full house.
It means Mother Hubbard being a grave robber
cloaking herself in hood and cape dark as her act.
This is what one does when one has dogs to beware of:
Dig up the prize begonias, a femur, fibula, a tibia, phalanges.
She didn't even love these bones when they walked the earth
in her man.

All it takes is faith
the size of a mustard seed that makes a real princess
toss and turn all night though it's under thirty mattresses.
I've never felt the wedding cake beneath my pillow,
the hard slice is now an artifact archaeologists attach
to a Jurassic Behemoth.

No better time to recall God's fascination
with his image. He put something of himself
in every creation. When he was tired
he made lazy idiots. When he had hiccups
he made tumbleweeds. When he needed a twin
he made Adam. And whenever he needed to
he watched Adam seduce Eve. And when once Eve refused
God's eyebrows raised, merged and flew off, a caracara
seeking carrion. And then there was wrath. *Vengeance
is mine* he said. And then there was his seduction
of Mary who had to submit, could not disobey the Lord.

If he told her he had not created disobedience
he lied.

Now the cyclone spirals above my house.
I vow not to go to heaven
if that's the only ladder.

SMALL CONGREGATIONS

Look around at Sis. Elden's brim wider than the arms
of the crucifix but without promises; looking
into her eyes is impossible so what could be found
there must be sought elsewhere, Tahlma Ollet's
keyboard-wide bosom always in tune (can't tell
she most died bringing a no-count into the world) unlike
the old spinet whose keys look perfect but don't deliver
the notes, the pitches. Then they come; Tahlma Ollet
shouts, from kitchen below us, the sound coming up
through water pipes and plaster, threadbare rugs that
the patting feet beat to death, a demon-killing stomp;
through our own feet whose tapping is an African
distress call probably but we're out of range, out
of touch, although you can't tell from the way Tahlma's
shout comes on up through our root system then out
of our own mouths though we're out of range of the
pepper, out of touch with the onions she's peeling
in the basement, holding for a moment,
before the knife enters,
a globe, a honey-colored moon, a cook's bible that she chops
into scriptures and makes us eat, tossing them
into every course: soup, entree, dessert.
Our shouting, our jubilation scares the ominous into
crouching behind our ribs where it intercepts what
would best serve us if it reached our hearts.

It does sometimes in the hint towards boogie-woogie
courtesy the tic in Elder Simpson's fingers, the
improvised pauses, hops, physiological product of
arthritis, spiritual product of faith, a holy rolling
of the eighty-eights when he plays *Sweet Home, T'is the
Old Ship of Zion*. Church starts to drift there,
crucifix, hand carved, painted brown, life size becoming

mainstay, frame of the storefront ark serving Mt. Pleasant,
home of urban schools named for dead white presidents.

Ushers pass out bread slice–shaped weighty paper
stapled onto tongue depressors, fans from the House of Wills,
funeral parlor, black owned and operated—some might say
death always was.
Not just grief shouts, not just fury rages.
Go, Willa, go; dance that holy dance, shake
those sinful tail feathers off! *Go on, Girl, shake*
that thing; go on, Girl, shake that thing! Let God
have his way, let the spirit take control, get up, get moving,
get on board; that's what Elder Simpson's playing now; *there's*
a train a comin'; tilt the cross and it's a railway crossing
sign; *a train's a comin'* just like yesterday, simply
switching tracks, from underground to the sky; freedom
still the destination, hear the stationmaster call: Cleveland,
Ottawa, Heaven—that's right, *Heaven;* not New Haven
    anymore!

WHEN I WAS 'BOUT TEN WE
DIDN'T PLAY BASEBALL

There's a wedding and I was not invited and that's
cool; what I would want to know, how pretty is
her dress, I can see from here. Not bad.
I like how the bride's all covered going into
the storefront church. She's made out like
an overcast day; she's saying: Probably not a good day
to picnic, rain likely, maybe heavy. She's not
honeymoon gullible. But then to the rescue, a man,
just when even fools who ordinarily do not give up
are giving up on sunshine,
lifts the veil and that strength always impresses me,
cause worry and doom and guilt are veils
that may as well be vaults the way they don't budge
even for optimism. Now they're man and wife.

Around the corner barbecue sweats on an oil-drum grill
in a parking lot where a Galaxie 500 wagon has
the tailgate down to make a Kool-Aid counter.
Slices of lemon swirl among ice cubes, the sugar
invisible, just an effect. It's hot. We might
sleep on the porch. Next year we really will have it
screened so we won't ever have to respect mosquitos
again. I listen to all the emergencies,
sirens of course, the Cadillac horns of the wedding, a mother
new to the area calling home her children
forgetting not to call the names of the ones who don't come
home anymore on nights like these when all it has to be
is summer and they're cared for better. The heat does hug.
It isn't shy and proper. My mother wouldn't want me
to play with it. There are ways to stretch, though; the moment
the hydrant's opened is just like releasing a rocket and then
we believe in water so much we jump in as it shoots, our clothes

becoming a new layer of skin sealing hope under it.
For a little while. That way, we don't get bored with hope.

Our fan is old. The motor talks too much, too loud, broods
and brawls. It has to be that way for anybody without
a lot of time left to get it all out. You have to talk out
your life so it won't be buried, just your bones that
can clackety-clack and yakety-yak after the flesh rots away
which it will faster if it's not holding onto life and won't
be none if you talk it out. Our fan's doing that. And
crickets talk back the lives they overhear. And it sounds so
good and perfect when they tell it, smooth and ideal, every
moment like a rocket blasting out of here to where we're not
supposed to go; way, way out of our league.

POEM FOR MY MOTHERS AND
OTHER MAKERS OF ASAFETIDA

Brown in the bottle, my
honeyed memory of my grandmother in
which I drench myself, pour over myself
one of her tight hugs, homemade gravy on
lips and ribs, eventually hips, *taste her, taste her*
and feast on my church in a bottle, the
gospel like Sis. Posey sings it, *oh when, when will
I get home?* Looking over Dixie, over
Jordan, river of life, needing to cross (already got
a cross), needing to swim to *Jordan's stormy
other shore,* listen: the brown choir's brown liquid voice,
my arms moving me through it, swimming is just directing
the choir, giving instructions, *Mama always told me to be still
sometimes and feel the power;* wait while the river moves down my
throat, urine the rest of the miracle that makes of me
a fountain; nasty asafetida, tastes like the bootleg, jackleg
medicine it is
curing me as only generations can, asafetida is *a quilt
for my innards,* she said, up to her neck in gizzards, hocks, pickled
pig's feet, her hands good as dull knives that can't
have accidents.
And everywhere, everywhere eggs like teeth big as
what memory does to Grandma. Even the heart of gold.

Finally
the asafetida toast just after gunfire, the new year
shot for coming uninvited, ahead of schedule, years
coming and going, out of control, Trojan years bringing
lots of what we don't want set loose in foreclosed fields
of stone potatoes so hardhearted, hardheaded there are
no eyes except the ones I look into and fall in love, right
into Mama's pupils, the past dark with dense ancestry, all

who came before having to fit into the available space of
history which is existence's memory and year after year
the overcrowding worsens, *remember; remember: darkest before
the day every dog will have,* we are dogs sometimes, vestiges
of our evolution giving us dreams, instincts, secrets for dark
recall; nothing really goes away
especially not that sickening paradox, falling to reach
the sublime emotion; want to rise in love, want a boost,
elevator ride to the penthouse, silk jacket smoking
with lust, man making it with an asafetida bottle, a glass
mama with an excuse for breaking; whatever sustains you is your
mama, that wall holding back wind, jazz on the airwaves and in
the Thunderbird, the Boone's Farm; the oar smacking discipline
into fish while ferrying you across the water
that takes you back to old Virginny, every visit is return
to the scene of crimes, so much happened there, so much history
there; rivers are sad affairs flowing between past and future
like pompous blue (if sunny) ribbons that must deepen, widen
or spill to really go anywhere and still there are limits,
disillusionment to cap any growth, live to the fullest and just
have more to lose to death but Grandma said, Mama says, now
I say: *maybe possible to have so much
death can't take it all;* asafetida still on the shelf, oil in the puddle
still ghetto stained glass, still rainbow remnants in rock
bottom ghetto sky like a promise of no more tears, asafetida
bottle floating there, some kind of Moses, some kind
of deliverer, there's always a way.
Away means not here. Place where bagpipes echo
with sound of a stuck doll calling *Mama, Mama,* nothing
but inspiration in the air, and the prophet Jolson
proclaiming *Mammy,* asking for her who can make him
wash his face; she's the one who can turn it into
something to love.

REMEMBERING KITCHENS

In the kitchen we compensate for missiles
in the world by fluting edges of crust
to bake rugged, primping rosettes and peaks
on cakes that are round tables with white
butter cloths swirled on, portable
Communion altars.

On the Sundays, ham toasted itself
with lipid melts, the honey veneer
waxed pork conceit to unnameable luster
and humps of rump poked
through the center of pineapple slices
so as to form tonsured clerical heads,
the Sundays being exceptional.

The waiting for the bread
helped us learn, when it arrived steaming
like kicked-up chariot dust then died down
quickly to the staid attitude of its brown dress,
the lovely practical.
In the center of the table
we let it loaf. When that was through
we sliced it into a file to rival the keeping
of the Judgment notes. So we kept our own,
a second set, and judged the judges, toasting
with cranberry water in Libbey glasses
that came from deep in the Duz. All this
in moon's skim light.

Somehow the heat of the stove,
flames shooting up tall and blue, good looking
in the uniform, had me pulling down the door,
the seat of the Tappan's pants, having the heat push

against me, melting off my pancake makeup, nearly
a chrysalis moment, my face registering then
at least four hundred degrees, and rising
in knowledge, the heat rising too, touching
off the sensors for the absolute mantra
of the ringing, the heat sizzling through cornices
and shingles, until the house is a warm alternative
to heavenly and hellish extremes,
and I remove Mama's sweet potato pie, one made
—as are her best—in her sleep when she can't
interfere, when she's dreaming at the countertop
that turns silk beside her elegant leaning, I slice it
and put the whipped cream on quick, while the pie
is hot so the peaks of cream will froth; these
are the Sundays my family suckles grace.

RAISING A HUMID FLAG

Enough women over thirty are at Redbones
for the smell of Dixie Peach to translate the air.
I drink when I'm there because you must have
some transparency in this life and you can't see
through the glass till it's empty.
Of course I get next to men with broad feet
and bull nostrils to ward off isolation.
You go to Redbones after you've been
everywhere else and can see the rainbow
as fraud, a colorful frown.
The best part is after midnight
when the crowd at its thickest raises
a humid flag and hotcombed hair reverts
to nappy origins. I go to Redbones
to put an end to denial.
Dixie Peach is a heavy pomade like
canned-ham gelatin. As it drips
down foreheads and necks, it's like tallow
dripping down candles in sacred places.

TWO

RUNNING OUT OF CHOICES

This is not about Beirut or El Salvador or Nicaragua,
words that get automatic respect
whether or not the speaker has anything to say.

I will not, therefore, mention Afghanistan, Poland
or Cambodia, not even the name of a favorite Chinese restaurant
for fear you might imagine the faces of Viet Cong peeping out
from the fried rice or little shipwrecked slant-eyed soldiers
floating towards shore on the tea bag in your cup.

I cannot even say Mississippi because someone might recall
that Medgar Evers was murdered there.

For related reasons I can't consider Alabama
unless I also consider churches and Easter dresses so ugly
bombs were thrown to eliminate the ugliness
while the girls were still in them.

Atlanta leads only to more bodies, some that didn't even
see puberty, never had sex, had never even been told about sex,
thought their own children would simply spring
from the split heads of cabbages on their mothers' counters
as their own split heads rot in gardens and dumps
making it possible to say that no burials are decent.

That kind of massacre, that kind of killer
makes me think the wrong babies are being aborted
—and love's deepest seed may be guilt.
No one's surprised, not even that Marvin Gaye, Sr.,
has slain Marvin Gaye, Jr., in *Los Angeles:* city of mercy,
city of angels.

I have no choice but to go home to Cleveland, *Evergreen*
cemetery, my father, Rebecca Robinson, Sis. Winchell
who killed her husband; Cordia Jackson, my pastor's daughter,
murdered in the projects, lye-based relaxer
in her short hair, other chemicals in the toilet;
at her funeral was the woman with whom Cordia's father,
the pastor, had an affair, and also present, another
preacher, father of the young man who was my only temptation
during a marriage tougher than temptation
despite a kettle-black girl imported from Jamaica
whom my husband found temporarily more exotic
than my blend of nigger and redskin;
back to my mother's picture window, bandaged with tape
where the bullet entered, only this time
it wasn't Kennedy's head

and now I'm in Texas, the Lone Star State
although the state of loneliness is unbearable; my star
is an asterisk on the roster to emphasize minority presence,
my star is in the constellation Pisces, the fish, the symbol
of Christians fed to lions, the symbol of healthy diets.
I want long life, I want eternal life so
I go to Communion service, I drink the blood, I eat
the broken body but the skimpy meal doesn't settle
on my stomach, it rises like Jesus.

Could this happen in Miami or is that place too infested
with foreigners like Haitians? Everyone likes to say *Haiti*
because it gives hate a proper home

and if a proper home is the idea
then it's back to Cleveland where every day
there's more news coverage than toothpicks.
Sometimes I want to give reporters a piece of my mind,
not answers to ill-conceived, inconsiderate questions
but they might not give it back

and I'm selfish, I want everything that's mine,
the auction block, the war bonnet, Mr. T's wreath of chains,
the right to vote politicians out of office, the ashes
of burnt crosses to scatter like ugly rumors, the black
market because white markets don't sell mocha-colored makeup
except in summer when white people want tans more than
they don't want to be black.

Where can I go and mention Big Dan hoping to discuss
Daniel Boone's contributions to society and not
a New Bedford gang rape?

Where can I go without somehow returning to Cleveland,
Evergreen cemetery, my father, Rebecca Robinson,
Sis. Winchell who killed
her husband, Cordia Jackson, my pastor's daughter, murdered
in the projects I might have lived in had I not been so lucky.

TIMEX REMEMBERED

In the middle of an argument I recall a high peak
in the South Pacific; a diver wearing
only loin cloth and watch
plunges, surfaces, thrusts his watch towards the camera
and microphone, then John Cameron Swazey takes over:
Timex, it takes a licking and keeps on ticking!

By fourth grade lickings simmered in everything
simmering. Dennis raped his sister's Patty Playpal
at her request. I locked my doll away. Olivia jumped
from a window the same day I saw a boy killed fifty yards
from a hospital, his bubblegum like a pink hole in
the street. What would he do, I asked the policeman,
without a sweet taste forever on his tongue?
I was pushed aside into silence, thereafter moved
through Glenville like a spirit.

It didn't make sense when Tomasina's mother whipped her
up and down Durkee Avenue with a peach tree limb.
Tomasina had done what her mother did, slept with a man,
someone else's man. Tomasina got a licking for her efforts,
her mother got Tomasina. And yes, Tomasina kept on ticking;
the cross around her neck moved like a metronome
when she walked.

Then there was Blondell who stole my piggybank full
of silver dollars, the only pieces of my grandmother
and her mother that I had. Blondell who stole
my innocence and couldn't even use it in her gang
that stole forty automobiles and dissected them.
She knew no other science. She popped her gum and
ticked like a bomb.

Louise thought her Navaho heart ticked too loudly
and I was so quiet she couldn't hear me above the racket
saying what I also needed someone to say.
She returned to Piñon, Arizona, in pieces
that each bore the signature of the craftsmen
who broke her with knives, bottles, and the tines
of forked tongues. *How* she said to me, *This is how*
she thought my silence said. I was praying
for the answer. Nothing ticks between us.

The lickings haven't stopped. Nowhere in the world
have the lickings stopped.
What else translates as well as the sun
setting in a bloodbath? Every heart bleeds
just keeping us alive. Oh the ticking, ticking. . . .
Sometimes that's just Old Lady Samodale trying
to grow flowers, not even thinking about race, not even
worrying about who's winning the human race, just doing
her spring cleaning, making room in her mind for flowers.
Rowdy youth ride by after a riot and tell her
the neighborhood is a ghetto now, no longer zoned
for the flowers they trample, uproot, try to smoke.
Their afros remind her of barbed wire. She knows more
about ghettos than they ever will. Her daffodils
were the goal of crayons. Sometimes the ticking
is Mrs. Samodale sinking to her knees, shaking *tch, tch, tch*
out of her head a long way from Czechoslovakia.
There's no freedom anywhere from the *Timex* watch, the
accuracy of its score.

FOR THOSE WHO CAN'T PEEL
THE POTATOES CLOSE ENOUGH

1.

Blondell, who engraved Bridgett's face with my nails,
looks cherubic in photos from my five-candle party:
bluish skin, paler ruffles and a tight blue rose
at the dropped waist of her dress.
She was the landlord's daughter, thirteen and
convenient; she was my sitter.
Sometimes the only payment she'd accept
was three White Castle burgers; she was a godsend
and so were plagues.

With my eyes closed I still see her
offering a choice of knife or her younger brother.

The night before Bridgett went back to Milwaukee
Blondell bound her in the basement with choice of
        heated
flat iron or Blondell to kiss.

I remember most the courtesy, Blondell's thank-you
when her brother turned to zip and cry.

2.

When Jesus was thirty-three
he began his work for the kingdom.
Scorpions tasted his heels
as he crossed the desert in a mirage,
walking to death as to a lost brother.

He always knelt on his shadow.

Now I am thirty-three
and sometimes unable to feel my right leg,
a numbness threatening my feeling
the best part of marriage, numbness
I first felt biting through haddock
and my lower lip until blood spurted
and I stopped at red as I always do.
The waitress did not and pocketed
the bloody money.

A red carpet is a tongue of blood.
Jesus never married.
I never French kiss.

3.

My first son is called Dennis
after my lawless brother-in-law,
after Blondell's brother.
He completes an anti-trinity.
Because he is black, he will think
he deserves this.

4.

Mrs. Arnstein doesn't know I listened
to her in the middle of the night.
With my fingers in my ears I housed
her crying in my head.
Together we watched smoke rising
over the harbor. "That's him," she said.

The Aryan woman on the box of Blue Bonnet
Mrs. Arnstein was loyal to is as excited about oleo
as I would be about ceasefire.

5.

Skylines graph rising courtesy
and are shrines to Blondell.
The story of her sainthood is the story
of the stone at the foot of a beach,
washed daily, gleaming as with holy oil
when the water recedes
as the Red Sea did,
as the flood did,
skeletons in their wake.

Medusa that Blondell was
she knew better than to look at herself
so her transformation to stone leads me
to conclude the miraculous visited.
Blessed rock, holy rock, a definitive prayer.
I can put my faith in such objects.
See, I throw one
and Blondell walks on water
before she drowns.

6.

All this is to show how we
are not a godless nation.
Those who can't peel the potatoes close enough
are not doomed. Look around. Some beaten women
stay in love because Jesus stayed on the cross.
The rhythm of belts finds a refrain in church bells.
Monastic silences govern many marriages. A jackhammer
makes a pentecostal call to worship. Tough saints
like Blondell beat us into submission, into clay
God can use to reshape us.
The method of salvation doesn't matter.
Let us receive the gun's sacrament, bullets
made of petrified bits of two-thousand-year-old body
followed by the siren's benediction.

APPROACHING VENUS'S-FLYTRAP
DURING A HUNGARIAN FILM:
A SUBTITLE

I assume hunger motivates the plant
past botanical limits. I should learn
from this, just wake up, out of hunger
for life, Caucasian or male, speaking,
for instance, the Hungarian the television
sneaks (it can get in what nothing else
can) into a room. There are subtitles

to make me doubt my ears, discourage
my own interpretations, fuck up
the possibilities of truth.

Hunger when it gets past cycles
of adolescent interest in gratification
forces martyrs. There is famine
when there's likely a shortage of saints.
Venus's-flytrap is naive. That name
is fake. A runaway on the Strip soliciting
flies, scavengers. Everyone else wears repellent.
The trick: hinged leaves, fringed like obviously
fake lashes, wink snug around insect bodies,
the plant working, surviving; for want
of the nitrogen fix the roots could just suck up
at home if the plant grew in one of those indulged
neighborhoods, a public display of what looks suspicious
like pleasure. Maybe none of us know.
Because we wait for the blossom;
we have a preference for puberty.
We cut them then.

I assume that the boys, running through
the movie's train towards the only woman
with a hat of black straw, nothing else
anywhere of black straw as if that hat
came from the last black straw in the world
so she is somehow the one all must run to
till the boys see someone easy to shoot;
I assume the boys are talking about that meat-
eating flower, how the devouring and violence
does not harm the greenness of
their similar innocence; I assume

that the subtitles are lies and necessary.

THE MANNA ADDICTS

1.

Manna must be pried from the road.
A boy helps me and we're a couple:
mother/son, father/daughter, lovers.
The mind is made to accept so much, truth
we couldn't possibly verify
except to point out new hairs around
my nipples. All growth will have to come
from within. These rocks are not unlike
the puffball cakes I sprinkled sugar over
on holidays.

2.

We pile manna on my skirt.
I'm ashamed only of not being much
to look at. Once I dreamt of stripping
in front of Hajek's Bakery, lying prone
on hot cobblestone until officers
covered me with a sheet.

The boy thinks only of manna,
should we eat it raw or cooked?
Should we save some and that way
make it inexhaustible?
I give him a piece, he won't swallow it
in this time of plenty. He can't remember
ever having more, not in the last hundred years.
He'd forgotten how long he'd lived, how much
he'd eaten: can't die or starve.
He throws the manna, hands me my skirt.
There's something eternal at work,
not the long-sought peace but   absence.

3.

We sketch birds in the dirt,
stare at them till they fly away
then we thank any idea of God that remains
in the rubble of St. Andrew's, holding hands
so tightly we break the nails; *yes,*
we were good parents, he tells me, staring
at the empty sky, *we let go.*

He leads me to the fishmonger's stall:
interpreter, tour guide, seeing eye,
composer of epitaphs.
Here, steel-and-brick-hued carp shined
like new money. That's when you buy,
after the ice under them melts, after
they stink. A good price then.

He spins a wheel of the overturned cart,
starts the monger's steely voice.
"Love for sale." *Buy it,* I plead.
"Going once." *Buy it.* "Going twice."
"Gone."

4. *Final Observations*

The couple who has everything
leaves the stall, hugging
the stinking parcel, passing it
between them. From a distance they're like
hosiery seams on a bowlegged woman.
After sunset they pale
into the thinnest glass,
weigh less than reflections.
Small crucifixes on filigree chains
fall through them.

TOY STOVE

He made it on the longest day
of the kindest metal

with hands that also stretched
dough as if to make it clutch
the frontal and zygomatic bones
of the gingerbread babies he exacted.
None aborted.

Sometimes his fingers streaked pink
and he lay down a horizon by his wife.

He made it electric.

Heat comes through four sets of circles
and warms six inches of air.

An egg eventually fries, the yolk
swirled in like a depthless vortex
and white invests the liquid window
of albumen, attaches it to a latex pump.

Four more sets of circles guide heat
to the oven that does not rush a cake,
the layers in the lids of cow-adorned
canisters took all day to bake, and were
sliced with a paper knife cut from the outline
of Mr. Arnstein's arm and hand.

No waiting for icing, no risking
the cooling of zeal; while the center

was hot we bit into textures that looked
knitted and called it purl cake

and the handmade sweater I called wool
cake, thinking I always would.

NIGGER FOR THE FIRST TIME

Bam! Nigger *turns the light off.*
Whoa! Stars astonish.

You are inspired.
You want to do what you've lately dreamed of,
put the cake on the phonograph turntable and
tape a spatula to the tone arm for automatic icing,
Nigger! you say; now that's just icing
melting, weeping on the cake.

It came from beautiful lips,
spittle on them like dew, another morning
unerring. From deeper than the throat
as if on the first attempt it had snagged
on ribs. It was not big; light and dabbed
on by someone used to perfume.

Hearing it, I became aware
of all the reverences, the bleats
of full lambs saying it too.
And my mother's feet anointed
with that word, resting on the lavender
cellophane of Easter baskets
for which she'd dipped pears in
chocolate.

There was a man by a river
limited in his idea of crossings
until he noticed water swishing brown
in its currents, the rapids serving up
fifties-times chocolate malteds

and he was gone home, and civil rights
were just gone, and nostalgia let him wade; he
could not drown in water *color of a perfect nigger,*
he said, *baby born knowing bear.*

THE BEST OF THE BODY

for Robyn

1. *Spleen*

It is highly vascular, that is
to say gifted; of the superior range
and more, no one is smart enough
to test its limits. No one
is God; God is not God.

The spleen is at the cardiac end
of the stomach, a fine neighborhood
patrolled by lymphocytes, white or colorless
nucleate cells that maintain immunity
to infection and resistance against bacteria
and other foreign entities except euphemisms.
O marvelous reservoir of blood,

red collection so gaudy it is fetish.
Worn-out erythrocytes the spleen destroys
and therefore eventually all the household
cells that submit to local drudgery, the carrying
of oxygen and hemoglobin they can't keep, and that's
how you get black bile, the melancholy next to mirth.

2. *Liver*

This is all the advice M____ could manage
when they came for Ethyl:

Don't hold it in your hand for it could be
drunk and not responsible and using that cover.
Beware the liver fluke, it is nothing but mistake,
nothing but parasite. Remember that the liver
does everything in the name of metabolism,

everything it does for Bolsheviks, for Nazis
and punks.

You will still be Ethyl when they call you C_2H_5OH
and send you to the liver. Do not be easy; you
owe that to womanhood, so wreck what you can.
To think that the first time you leave home
it's a little trip to the system.
Darling Ethyl, readiness has never mattered.

3. Heart-to-heart Talk
—Have a heart and a nice day.

*—Thank you. I have put the heart
in my mouth; is that the right place?*

—Here; how about a change of heart?

*—No; I haven't quite finished this one
on my sleeve.*

*—So it's that way, is it? I suspect
you're after my own heart.*

*—Oh no; you know I don't have the heart
to do that. You know me by heart; remember?
Please believe me; I'm swearing with all my heart.*

*—Really? Well, I believe that came from
the bottom of your heart, close to the dregs,
the liver and spleen, not the creamy brain.*

CHA-CHA PICKLE

If the cha-cha pickle fails
the way I did learning the icehouse
then heaved and heaved all night
a good part of the devil out of me;

if the cha-cha pickle fails
and the wheat still goes under the blade
without so much as a *baa,* and then under
the weather, troubled roses of the wall cloud
letting down their stems, funnels of love,
to screw what screwed them;

if the cha-cha pickle fails
to burn, what will dance
the dinner down?

    Shouldn't that be chow-chow pickle?
Sure, in the best of all worlds,
not a town all focus and spotlight,
blue to see lice.

Planned was a trip to nostalgia
that I was too young for
including reverence for the creek
that wouldn't drown my father, its
cottonmouths coiled and stacked so that
he bounced out dry.
That was the only time he swam.

The icehouse's cold translucent towers
just wouldn't turn ivory
and though I brought smoke, they
didn't catch on, remained impossible

to defile; their clear melt, my red gore.
Those were to be my building blocks, my
chance at igloo, but I couldn't make an igloo
be what I thought it was.

Down south, the white bathrobe around me
pure fleece casement doing no good
on this night of nights' access to Miss Helen's
indoor tub opaque as the teeth of those
who rhymed my name with *Dallas* and made it mean
Dallas in the honky-tonk where I saw and heard
things I still won't do or say
even in Dallas. The very next day

I got my very first bra and so much caution
the world was replaced with a preference
for burning available in Mason jars of cha-cha
pickle taking over the icehouse and justice
as would storms.

DEAR CHARLES

You really didn't have to blow me a tornadic kiss all the way to Michigan. Why do you think I'm going in January when the cold holds you back and I can delay kissing you back until spring? Your kisses, your troubled, spinning roses tearing down the door, breaking the windows, taking it all by force while I say *no*. You heard me correctly all right; I'm going to Michigan, to the midwest breeding ground of these plants, to the industrial heart and smokestacks belching their labor of love: dark bouquets, little funnel clouds, hollow cornucopia. I used to think those factories manufactured the storms, that they were showing off just like the boys I knew who named their Huffys "Bronco." I never blamed God for tornadoes; his were mysterious ways, and nothing is less mysterious than a tornado's system of rage. I'm going to Michigan as if to chase the tornado, corner it, force it into a bottle and have a dark form of lava lamp that gives off no light. This is not a good attitude towards power, but it is the one that I have and the one that will get me to Michigan with my *no* vocabulary intact.

A few years ago I tracked a hurricane for the first time. It is as if I came east just to do this. You can imagine how shocked I felt when all that macho flexing turned out to be your routine. You still swear by it, but that's not the way to get me in bed with you. If you hadn't knocked down the lines and cables, you would have heard the songs: "Try a Little Tenderness" and "Slow Hand." You were an assailant, not a lover. The hurricane is all wind, fucked-up clouds and unholy water spinning like a Ninja weapon, flung at the coast like a Ninja weapon. What I like about the Teenage Mutant Ninja Turtles is the mutancy, the assurance of aberration, the likelihood of extinction since most mutants are sterile. Not Charles though, who, male and all, gives birth to tornadoes; little pieces of him drop off and spin madly. Mutant dervishes? Proof that Charles is neurotic and hip? Is he mocking the hula? Is he jealous and retaliating by cross-dressing, putting on a wind skirt? Could he be trained for meaningful service instead of riot? How about adjunct windmill?

How about head adjunct windmill? Sterile or not, Charles is not the man for me or anyone. He is not a lady's man, not a man's man. Not even three-fifths of a man. Forgive me, but the way I feel, I can deal with you only in the third person, which is the same as dealing with the Third World. Disaster will never be natural. You can stop auditioning for the Beast, a part already cast and transformed. Everything's mangled, even the land, chewed up, spit out; if you're going to ask for it, at least you should clean your plate. Didn't your mother teach you anything?

You are one rude son of a bitch. A sociopath if I ever saw one. I'm not going to hold my breath waiting for an apology, but you really ought to learn to hold yours. Just where do you get off messing over a whole city? But that's the game plan, isn't it? You are a gang storm. One big fat swirl of attitude. A supreme macho feast in the midst of wrecked appetite. What can you say but, "Excuse me, I was abused as a child"?

Charles's reply:

Baby, you know I was abused as a child. You can't erase history. It started soon after Africa birthed me. At first I was just depressed, just feeling some colonial effects. I went for a walk, then I went for a swim to clear my head and gain some perspective, and I found myself on Gorée Island. Them currents started some tough pulling, Jack! I just couldn't resist. The influence came down like a Jones; I was feeling the thousands who were bound and chained right where I was. Okay? That stuff turned me into a storm; everything about me became a layer of maelstrom; I ain't had no more eyes, mind; nothing to direct me but justice. And, see; there weren't no chains holding me back and making inability to act seem like consent. You know Charles ain't no kind of proper African name, but it's the one my patrons give me, the one meteorological overseers picked out. If they had just bothered to respect my tribe, I might have toned down a notch. I ain't confused or nothing; I know I'm not a slave, so I'm not for sale, but I am owned, and payment is due on the privilege of having me.

Yours,

BEANSTALK DREAMS

At first I was inside my man; the twisting
sinews and muscles overlaid carefully as
bandages provided footholds. In the night

he had grown around me. First
our legs intertwined, then his arms took on
willow ways and I did not resist the branches

despite being thoroughly girled in my youth.
This part was no dream, just the way after
twenty years beside him that sleep must be

induced. Sometimes when my head is on his
chest, I share his beard as soft scrolled
hairs work themselves into my cheek like pointed

kisses. In that position we watch the parade of
gaunt images on an old Motorola; black and white static
whining in attraction, whining in denial, duplicated

by the friction of our hands heating up a backrub.
When the vertical hold dissolves, the rolling
is that of the old knickknack man coming home.

For me however there is the detour of
my husband's mouth, his tongue as dependable as
a Swiss cuckoo keeping track of the bliss of hours.

In the sweetish scent of burnt Jerusalem jasmine
there is evidence of holiness in our love's orthodoxy
although the ritual's passion seems

to have other than heavenly sponsor
in its lack of modesty or inhibition,
which is often the last barrier to temptation

and was still standing after the walls of Jericho,
stands still after Berlin. What giant awaits
when I reach the top? Do I become the monster

when I assume godly heights without godliness
to help me handle where I am? This upper air
and the northern seas feel right and the same,

cold, cold zealots. What a wasteland can be
the fixed and frozen smile. But there
are golden eggs to shine and hatch. There

is a harp and a lyrebird. There is milk
to separate from honey and to purify. In
the middle of the night, my husband is at

my breast where the baby used to be and
despite everything, he has spared me the
trauma of weaning, of shrinking, of having

good feelings grow too thin to believe
making the mind as infertile as my body
must become unless I am less than woman.

No; I have not yet climbed down and the ax,
the ax—why, there's no such thing
as an ax.

THE SUGAR SLAVE

Once upon a time a little boy felled a tree
that nobody heard in the Dominican Republic or
in Haiti where he was purchased for what usually
is an hour's wage in Texas and everywhere north
that has these lovely crystal jars, crafted
to catch light in ways that exaggerate breakfast,
filled with sugar, perhaps Domino brand (Freudianly
named for a certain effect), perhaps not, but likely
from the forest of cane the boy chopped down.

> *He must therefore be superhuman.*
> *He must therefore live in a fairy tale.* Why

the machete is as long as his legs! He's
only eight. By the time he is thirty-eight
his legs will be much longer, but the machete
will be bigger than his life.

> *This therefore is miraculous.*
> *This therefore remains a fairy tale.*

From the poorest island he has been snatched
into comparative paradise, Dominican paradise.
So, so sweet an opportunity. He will have a room
and six others will have it too. And he will have
all the cane (and only cane) he can eat and eat and
he cannot possibly eat it all. He will have no toilet
(not that he ever did); the pee will snake
through the cane which will be even sweeter.

> *Therefore the cane is enchanted.*
> *Therefore this is a fairy tale.*

The boy gleams in his sweat like the knight cutting
through thicket and briars to wake at precisely
the right moment the one getting her beauty sleep
or she wouldn't be beautiful, a cake, too soon
from the oven, that although young droops and sags
like the old woman no one wants to become, a cake
with the sugar extracted, with silicon substitutes
and other lifts, tucks, and preservatives.

> *Therefore mirror mirror hype.*
> *Therefore mirror mirror hope.*

The boy cuts through miles and years of cane.
When something is as beautiful as the promise
the sun makes every morning when the cane
seems a garden of golden flagpoles marking independence,
end of colonialism, he would try to kiss it if
his mouth had not been ruined. He bites deep
into the raw form.

> *He bites the fairy tale in two.*

He bites into what hypnosis wants to take you to
so you can understand hatred denied, repressed,
refined and in the jar you pass upon request.

SPILLED SUGAR

I cannot forget the sugar on the table.
The hand that spilled it was not that of
my usual father, three layers of clothes
for a wind he felt from hallway to kitchen,
the brightest room though the light bulbs
were greasy.

The sugar like bleached anthills of ground teeth.
It seemed to issue from open wounds in his palms.
Each day, more of Father granulated, the injury spread
like dye through cotton, staining all the wash,
condemning the house.

The gas jets on the stove shoot a blue spear
that passes my cheek like air. I stir
and the sugar dissolves, the coffee giving no evidence
that it has been sweetened and I will not taste it
to find out, my father raised to my lips, the toast burnt,
the breakfast ruined.

Neither he nor I will move from the shrine
of Mother's photo. We begin to understand
the limits of love's power. And as we do,
we have to redefine God; he is not love at all.
He is longing.

He is what he became those three days
that one-third of himself was dead.

THE PARTY TO WHICH WOLVES
ARE INVITED

I'm five years old.
My parents tell me I'll turn into a boy
if I kiss my elbow.
(I have a moustache
because I almost succeeded).

I like to hear them at night
trying to kiss their own elbows
and turn into each other,
she thinking to show him
what a husband should be,
he intending to teach her
a thing or two about wives.

When the moon gets full of itself
my parents do not make love.
We live in an attic. We make do.

Lightning flashes as night is executed.

I'd rather kiss toads.

Stormtrooping thunder arrives. Anne is doomed.

See Anne. See Anne run. Run, Anne; run to Burundi
where 95 of every 100 adults (and all of the children)
can't read or write or draw swastikas.

I knew it; I'm dreaming I lift violets to her nose.
She pots the scent in beer steins.

I go to summer camp in a Radio Flyer wagon.
I lift the violets to her nose. I kiss her elbow.
She's in my cabin. She can't swim either. We kiss
toads in the swamp. The graves are muddy bathtubs.
The toads turn into paterollers, sell us.
From the frying pan, Anne, into the fire. Next time
it will still be fire although my parents do not make love.
The moon is full of itself. Look at that yellow
skin; bet my bottom dollar the baby will be mulatto
but no one's on bottom, no one's on top; my parents
do not make love. *Runagate, runagate.* Keep moving.
Women and children first. Every man for himself. Kiss
the blood off my elbow, please. I'm homesick.
I send letters with no return address. I don't know
where I am, where the attic is.
All I know is that I smell violets.
I must be near the woods. Near wolves.
They have no elbows. I can kiss them all day long
and they won't turn into something else.

Surprise! My parents step out.

THE WONDER

Over my shoulder in Danbury, Connecticut, as I drove,
my father came back to wipe the rear window
and I could see, more clearly behind me than
in front, his one Studebaker dream but couldn't
smell the bakery in that so we walked from then on,
full of the smell; that was the wonder
of Wonder bread—we didn't have to buy any.

THE WAKE FOR THE LOST TWO
HUNDRED MILES

It was August, the summer ritual
was mandatory so we were going
and he was wise not to say where
back when the fuel had names, Ethyl
and Boron. *Give me, Boron*
he would say reminiscing Neanderthal
and doing a sophisticated Tarzan
(*Boron* is one syllable up on *Jane*)
at the same time. Just half a tank
so we'd have to fill twice as much
and meet twice as many Joes.

The attendants were always tall and lean.
They posed like dirty blue cigarettes
against the pumps, waiting for the gallons
to roll by like credits and looking for
their names. I didn't have to read their names
in the red-rimmed, oil-smudged ovals; it was
Joe or Jack, Sam or Mack until much, much later
way down the road.

The main highways were paved slick as Elvis;
we avoided those so his wheels could crack gravel,
build church.

The hose and car and pump
were hooked up together like a woman
to the curling apparatus that did
poodle-dos. That wasn't why you went.

Joe raised the hood, diddled with
the dipstick, stroked carburetor

like fetish which it is.
Then he did the circle job on the
windshield with his hands and a cloth
until the glass was clean, new, yet didn't
disappear; there was glare, the sunburst
effect, definitely not absence. Through
all this, talk was the clock obeyed.
Afterwards Joe opened the pop machine,
with a silver key like an ankh, tossed
one Patio orange to my father, drank
one himself, got me purple slush.
A supper of cold beans and a tomato
sandwich, a three-way split and we all
thought to ourselves: We've got
the three monkeys, three stooges, even
the trinity covered.

DEATH OF THE SWEET WORLD

She can't eat salt or sugar,
the sweet world is gone, the sour
and bitter remain.

When my mother dies
she'll want me to style her hair,
touch the embalmed cheek, slip a ring
my father meant to buy on her finger.

She'll want me to sit on her grave
and write poems there as if what I lack
is influence.

What will happen to the rooms
she used to clean,
the wealthy widows who asked her
to iron perfect linens
and had tables set for two, coffee steaming
when she arrived?
I once told her to get a decent job.

Those houses were cleaner than her own;
she didn't mind dirt, the dust so much
like ashes of loved ones.

Her heavy perfume scented
the early morning with olfactory fog.
I walked through it hours later
going to school.

The bags she carried made her look homeless.
So did the coats and stretch pants of widows.

She was in charge
of all the church's books
except the Bible, preferring the one
she had at home; in it
Jesus's words are red.

When she said grace
her hands swept across the meal
as if she was in love
with the broom.

HOLDING

Nobody knows about the wig
and she doesn't look at herself
taking it off. Then she feels
for her own stubby braids, unbraids
them, liking the coarseness
like a working man's hand. It's been so long
simulation will do just fine, thank you.
But not liking it enough.
The wig is smooth.

She braids them again, obeying
a tradition in Ghana, in Guinea
in a D.C. home business where thousands
of women are queens for days and days
when they leave, for the braids last and last.

She tucks the stubby braids under a tight-
fitting crown, a stocking cap. Then
she talks to God, getting down on her knees
as if the room is full of smoke.

The God she pictures is white headed, his eyes
are oceans, his muscles are trees; his knuckles,
mountain ranges; there are escarpments
where the cuticles drop down to nails, valleys
between his toes, and a pot belly
for the fat of the land
and that is how he holds the whole world.
He need not speak; she trusts him
to put her on hold too.

She sleeps well. She holds her dreams well
although she is asleep, her grip does not weaken.

THE LINOLEUM RHUMBA

On parade: some of the dancer's many personalities and
guises, the Nelsons' cook, the Peabodys' domestic,
the geriatric ward's bed pan handler and

her children: child of the babushka, child of
the do-rag, child of the scarf, child of the veil,
child of the wig, child of the tortilla, child of
pita, child of hominy, cornpone and grits.

Some think she's going to shine the podium and
it's true that her bosom dusts it as she speaks:

I left Mississippi for Toledo.
I left Toledo for Watts.
Thought I would see light, but
we can't stay here, we can't live this way
all by instinct but not the instinct
bred in Toogaloo and fed Pearl water.

What my children need are commando strategies that
you'd think being who and what I am I would have.
My sour lemons are the most like grenades but
they make our mouths pucker and all we can talk about
then is brotherly love.
I've also got diamonds and spades, hearts and clubs
that I keep passing out to my young ones but Lord
if my eldest doesn't keep throwing his on the table.
I don't want him shot, so I let him shoot nothing,
not the breeze, not a family picture, not hoops.

Let me clear up a nagging misunderstanding: This
is the way to make the white woman's bed; she thinks

*I make it because she is rich, she thinks I make it
to get her money, that I can't get money any other
way, no skills, no intelligence, no contribution to
society but for her four poster, but I make her bed
because on judgment day, you will have to sleep
in the bed you made and I make damn good ones but
she didn't make any.*

Enter the cat pawing its way out of the bag and into
the cathouse on Catfish Row, no story completely believed
without nasty black women, their shortchanged alphabet,
from D to W, domestic to whore, sheets binding them, their
fishnet stockings hooking innocent men trying to be disciples
or they wouldn't be studying no net.

Know what she does? Goes right on loving that man limb
by limb, the mop right out of a stick figure drawing
and something to smile about: *only the flesh is weak and
ain't none of that on him nowhere.* They're
going out tonight, a heavy date, even dancing.

Sunday finds her on the mourner's bench. The song
closes in on her: *Oh, loose that man and let him go.*
Then she knows; her mop is the rib, staff of Moses, spigot
for the rock water coming then, from her clay heart, her
Mississippi mud face, tributary with Niagara destiny cutting
to the bone, leaping from chin to breast
where it works its way back in

and she feels renewed, as if she's just slapped
Master's fresh face, ruddy as the cut flowers
brought in this morning to grace the altar
she'd swept clean of petals, flower crap, rose
and carnation doo doo.

She returns to the podium, kicks the cat off
the platform, speaks: *Children, ain't a damn thing to
be sorry for this morning.*

The huge crowd doesn't know what to do as
they've come resolved to apologize.

RUSH HOUR

He boards the train downtown,
same time I get on in Lee Heights.

Eastbound passes westbound.
Can't pick him out,

square-shouldered every one of them,
under 40 years old, over 40 thousand a year,

never glancing up from their papers
till they pass Quincy, Central Avenue's

gutted brownstones, record and head shops,
Joe D's Tavern where I rent the back room.

He's ashamed of what we have in common.
I just left his house. Spotless.

ONE-LEGGED COOK

A high school cafeteria
is where I work. "Hop to it, Velma,"
kids say when the line moves slow.
My son eats outdoors from a bag,
collar turned up, napkin
covering his knees.
That's what I live with.
Never occurred to me
I was missing out on something.
Though seldom seen in Culvert Hall
I know to sit still
when the conductor taps his stick;
my father waved a strap.
Besides, it doesn't take that much,
the burdock by the courthouse
grew an eighth of an inch
since yesterday.
A lot of folks didn't notice.

THIS MAGICIAN

From the hat once checked at Club 54
he pulls a sickly rabbit.
From circus to circus, benefit to benefit
the same rabbit. Bald spots
suggest the love and dependency of a child
on a mute, comatose and flammable toy
where in fact this magician has yanked,
fingernails like cleats through white gloves.

Sometimes this magician wears the mortician's
suit and nobody knows.

Sometimes this magician is Mr. McGregor
keeping rabbits out of his garden
so that it will win prizes.
The lesson of Eden.

Sometimes rabbits named Misha, Lottie,
David, yes, and Peter, every name in the book
were seized from hats, trains, piano recitals,
surgery, weddings, school.

It was unbelievable.
It was magic.
It was beyond the normal parameters
of the senses.
It was impossible to watch
yet who wanted to miss
the theoretically possible moment
that the sleight of hand might fail
so how it could be done
could be understood.

Flopsy, Mopsy and Cottontail were good
little bunnies, ate their bread and milk
and blackberries
in silence
in darkness
in hiding
and one summer day went to camp
as children do.

THE EYELID'S STRUGGLE

We watch the pigeons bring back
the crusts left on the curb, the stiff
contexts for rye centers. If news
were history we would still read the paper.
History tells us what is worth remembering.
Not Mother's postage stamp–sized obituary.
Grief for her would be wasted, she
did not start a war, she did not stop one.
She patted on powder two shades lighter than
her face, an inch of white lies that
rubbed off on her pillow. The lies
would not stay buried. White lies
are history, white lies are policy, broken
promises to Indians.

We need to know what happened
to the canteen that formed the base
of the lamp that vanished when
I turned it off. I couldn't find
the switch in the dark; I felt like a blind
woman choosing tomatoes and realized absence
of sight did not mean absence of prejudice.
Absence of prejudice is a white lie. Mother
wore absence of prejudice to bed; when
Father kissed her, it was on his lips.
The canteen used to hold water but we didn't thirst
in the daytime. We needed light more than water.
Overnight, though, dry dreams delivered dehydration,
soda cracker clouds cracked into Communion that
cut our tongues; that was the blood, not symbolic
wine; that was salvation, the scar tissue that
formed stops us from lying.

At my request he stopped calling me rabbit.
After that, batches of his hot slaw traveled
like lava from the kitchen. It seasoned
everything, made it taste the same.
It brought the absence of prejudice to
the palate, it burned the tastebuds, we ate
hell to eliminate it as an outcome. Above
our heads the cooing suggested immature lambs,
incomplete sacrifice. The flapping
was the eyelid's struggle with tears.
When one must learn about life from a
pigeon, one learns what hardened the crusts
in the first place. A dead rabbit
doesn't always mean new life will enter the
world, sometimes just
that something is gone, won't ever
be back, that you have killed.

SHE DID MY HAIR OUTSIDE,
THE WASH A TENT AROUND US

Right over left, left over right, Mama
disciplines braids. The Hair Rep melting
on her fingers irrigates my cornrows.
She sings *don't let this harvest pass you by*.
I struggle to stay a child but I hear her.
I'm between her knees and see myself as
Papa's overalls coming through the wringer,
Jewish flat bread. The Jewess is downstairs.
Logic postulated convergence of our lives.
Her songs burn me too, my hair steams
while the comb reheats.

Papa's name is Abednego.
He works with rubber.
He has become as waterproof as his tires.
Baptism beads off him. He and the Jewess
are in the same boat; too bad it's fire next time.
I'm on the masthead. I'm in his wallet, on
the Jewess's polished piano top. Framed.
The trip through the wringer superimposes me
on sensitive paper. Caring paper. Jew-skin paper
on which you write love and kisses. Then you send it
through the wringer without letting go. Special
delivery. Mama's fingers are the woof of my braids.
Mooring. The same boat. Hair Rep river. Drifting
to roots. Kinky. Nappy. Textured. Mama's blind
and finds her way to me, rocking the boat,
rocking me in an autistic way that saves.

SHE'S FLORIDA MISSOURI BUT SHE WAS BORN IN VALHERMOSA AND LIVES IN OHIO

My mother's named for places, not Sandusky
that has wild hair soliciting the moon like blue-black
clouds touring. Not Lorain with ways too benevolent
for lay life. Ashtabula comes closer, southern,
evangelical and accented, her feet wide as yams.

She's Florida Missouri, a railroad, sturdy boxcars
without life of their own, filled and refilled with
what no one can carry.

You just can't call somebody Ravenna who's going
to have to wash another woman's bras and panties, who's
going to wear elbow-length dishwater to formal gigs,
who's going to have to work with her hands, folding and
shuffling them in prayer.

THREE

BIRMINGHAM BROWN'S TURN

I know how ridiculous this could seem, the
moon as one of Birmingham Brown's pop eyes when
he's admiring Charlie Chan as living

icon, but I can't stop seeing the magic, even
as Birmingham drives Charlie around
in a car black as Birmingham, black as

compliment, emulation, and adoration. Ridiculous
were it not wonderful, Birmingham's enormous
feel for the night, moving in it

like something made for it, made
of it; the city, every city wearing
his face at night, his smile a

handy lantern—ooh; marvel at those skyscrapers
that pushed up from underground like
flowers; their office lights

come on like petals opening, the
cleaning ladies there like bees
busy pollinating, pulling buckets

of nectar with umbilical arms, honeying
the floors till the sweet glow
pops out, a girlish event, a knowing

and liking puberty's entitlement.
How can anyone who thinks the place
is one big apple understand? It's

a whole damned apple orchard! I
realize that Birmingham is supposed
to be insult, a debit not credit

to his race; we're just ashamed
that his costume and mask fit so
well, as if we believe that clothes

make men, but hear this and hear this
well: no polyester, no rayon or
Charmeuse blouse is my creator. And

consider; his performance—according
to script, not autobiography by the way—
did not lower the bottom-hugging black

race. And anyway, what if
the world—knowing how crazy it is
documented to be—is traveling upside

down; what if Birmingham is on the
top? The night sure treats him
royally; he glides through it as though

in a coach; it sure pampers him, opens
itself so that walking towards you
he disappears before reaching you; the

night, a woman dark, passionate, heavy with
her love, pulls him into her secret
chambers, won't give anyone a chance at

taste. I don't know names, never had to
consider nationality, just race; black is black
everywhere in the world. Dark moments,

pestilences tend to dominate our minds, stand
out like sentries though what they guard
is unclear. Despite this, *Ustinov* to me

sounds more Russian than *Georgia* that to me
is a conjure word summoning the cotillion
and pecan eyes, pies and earlobes; peaches

rushing to shave off what's just now
telling the world they're men. But authentic
Atlanta (accept no imitation) men have

a way of saying what they are that won't
let the world forget. I don't mind
the beard stuck on Ustinov, it seems

appropriate for his purpose:
effigy, caricature. And that broken English
tripping out his mouth appropriately

in bound footsteps. Now how would it look
for Charlie Chan not to be recognizably
Chinese especially when Ustinov cannot

draw from his rickshaw infancy, his
ideographic preschool scribbles, his
chopstick crutches to help him eat

moo goo gai pan, his first words, before
even *mamasan* or *papasan* or is that
Japanese? Who can tell just

by looking at his face, the Russian
stubble poking through to ferret out
Viet Cong, Viet anything, Hmong women

just as good, even Cambodian though
they can lean too Polynesian-looking so
back off, spare them. As for the rest,

see one, you've seen them all, hovering
above the number one son like a mist
to cool his face, so hot

under the makeup that upsets, tilts
his eyes. Appropriately. Asian eyes
being the claim to fame. And silk.

You can bet that Charlie can take you
to the cleaners; isn't he Chinese?
Don't they boil the clothes and the

rice in the same woks? Isn't this
the year of the horse, the broken,
tamed stallion? Of the Mongoloid

Idiot? Of Peking sitting duck? That's
what Charlie said, that's all he can say,
cliche after cliche, stereotype after stereotype

even when he's alone sleeping parallel with
his geisha (he says no matter what she really is),
together they're models for the railroad tracks,

just straighten the cross's horizontal arm,
lengthen both to infinity, crucify the same. . . .
Just the same, we come back, all the persecuted

and oppressed, even to ride if we must
chop chop trains instead of *choo choos*.
For they can move in and out of shadows cast

when a Hiroshima girl's thousand cranes
fly by the sun; their silhouettes
are exclamation marks. We turn it all around

and still dare to dream of it, digging to China,
going through the center of the earth's meaning
and potential to *earn,* to *deserve* passage there;

through the center and cleansed, wanting
that moment that worms complete their evolution
into egg rolls and dandruff is recycled into bait

that entices some junk boat occupants
to take us in because they're the ones
who walk on water all the time.

To hell with Peter, that's what Birmingham's
fortune cookie said; either one, Ustinov
or Jesus' right-hand man.

Going there, we notice how Jesus
can become Confucius without a hitch
and can keep his parables if he wishes.
We all keep salvation.

A LITTLE SOMETHING FOR
BUCKWHEAT AND OTHER
PICKANINNIES

Look at the kite strings of your hair
tied into knots like balls and chains.
Does Mammy know about this?

Some people have you (or your brother Farina)
for breakfast, drown you in milk, shower you
with cinnamon's rusty rain, dredge you
with a grainy web of sugar.

Sometimes you were a girl and ugly.
Sometimes you were a boy and ugly.

Buckwheat, I honor you
and what was explained as
African ways.

What did they know
of the comfort of a flour sack,
those who designed your costume,
seeking a match
for the discomfort assumed
you felt wearing your skin?

THE LYNCHING

They should have slept, would have
but had to fight the darkness, had
to build a fire and bathe a man in
flames. No

other soap's as good when
the dirt is the skin. Black since
birth, burnt by birth. His father
is not in heaven. No parent

of atrocity is in heaven. My father chokes
in the next room. It is night, darkness
has replaced air. We are white like
incandescence

yet lack light. The God in my father
does not glow. The only lamp
is the burning black man. Holy
burning, holy longing, remnants of

a genie after greed. My father
baptizes by fire same as Jesus will.
Becomes a holy ghost when
he dons his sheet, a clerical collar

out of control, Dundee Mills percale,
fifty percent cotton, dixie, confederate
and fifty percent polyester, man-made, man-
ipulated, unnatural, mulatto fiber, warp

of miscegenation.
After the bath, the man is hung as if

just his washed shirt, the parts
of him most capable of sin removed.

Charred, his flesh is bark, his body
a trunk. No sign of roots. I can't leave
him. This is limbo. This is the life after
death coming if God is an invention as were

slaves. So I spend the night, his thin moon–begot
shadow as mattress; something smoldering
keeps me warm. Patches of skin fall onto me
in places I didn't know needed mending.

LUNCHCOUNTER FREEDOM

I once wanted a white man's eyes upon
me, my beauty riveting him to my slum
color. Forgetting his hands are made for my
curves, he would raise them to shield his eyes
and they would fly to my breasts with gentleness
stolen from doves.

I've made up my mind not to order a sandwich on
light bread if the waitress approaches me
with a pencil. My hat is the one I wear
the Sundays my choir doesn't sing. A dark
bird on it darkly sways to the gospel music,
trying to pull nectar from a cloth flower.
Psalms are mice in my mind, nibbling,
gnawing, tearing up my thoughts.
White men are the walls. I can't tell anyone
how badly I want water. In the mirage that
follows, the doves unfold into hammers.
They still fly to my breasts.

Because I'm nonviolent I don't act or
react. When knocked from the stool
my body takes its shape from what
it falls into. The white man cradles
his tar baby. Each magus in turn.
He fathered it, it looks just like him,
the spitting image. He can't let go of
his future. The menu offers tuna fish,
grits, beef in a sauce like desire.
He is free to choose from available
choices. An asterisk marks the special.

THE DAY BEFORE
KINDERGARTEN: TALUCA,
ALABAMA, 1959

I watch Daddy tear down
Mama Lelia's outhouse
with just his hands;
the snakes and slugs
didn't fret him none.
Then he takes me and Mama riding.

We stop at the store,
looks like a house,
okra right in front,
chickpeas and hollyhocks.
Me and Mama go in. The fan
don't move her hair.
She keeps her head down, stands
a long time at the counter.
Just wants some thread,
could get it herself,
there's a basketful beside her.
Clerk keeps reading.

She's hurting my wrist,
I pull away, pick up a doll.
Clerk says we have to leave.
Mama grabs me and runs
right by Daddy,
he's just coming in.

We hide in the car.
Mama smells like sour milk
and bleach.

Daddy comes out toting a sack,
clerk thought he was white.

When the store starts burning
I'm on Mama Lelia's porch
wanting to see
how the red
melts off peppermint.
I know it's like that.
One by one
each thing burns.
Pickle jars explode.
Mama Lelia asks me:
Do it look like rain?
No'm, it don't.
Ain't God good!
She laughs.

Later,
while it's still smoking
I go poking with a stick.
Ashes look like nappy
nigger hair. Smells
like when the hot comb
gets too hot
and burns Mama's neck.
This smell's so big
must have come
from a hundred necks.

Holding my doll
I look at the smoke,
could be a black man
running down the road;
then rub some ashes
on her face

'cause I ain't scared
no more
of nothing.
Maybe I should be
but I ain't.

THE ROOT OF THE ROAD

My hem eats the dirt haunting
my footsteps with apparitions of flies.
The road is a tongue stretched speechless.
Were I trampled faceless, I would be this
road. Whenever possible I look for where
the mouth was, I lament its loss of hair, the
uselessness of my toes combing the dirt like
plows. My own hair hangs like old udders.
I am the milk bypass, the shortcut to hunger.

Mistress Jane, color of dough, twisted into fancy
bread, yeasty, floury, my hands when I bathe her.
She is not the one whose rising proclaims day.
She wants the road to Natchez when she looks at me,
my back doesn't disappoint. I don't feel her hand
when it touches my shoulder to guide it. What is
on me couldn't make itself felt though I wore it all
day like an epaulet. Even after removing my calico,
her glove, a layer of air prevailed, separating our skin.

My hands circled her neck following the road's
curve. Dust flew from her mouth disguised as
breath. Had she stayed mute she would have lived,
those words *after all I've done for you* (said also
to her mirror) buried me while I held onto her.
The displaced dirt from the hastily dug grave went
on walking the parent road as me. Mistress Jane was
quite comfortable underground with other roots.
Who besides the flies will believe I held a pink flower
by its pinker stem?

INTERPRETATION OF A POEM
BY FROST

A young black girl stopped by the woods,
so young she knew only one man: Jim Crow
but she wasn't allowed to call him Mister.
The woods were his and she respected his boundaries
even in the absence of fence.
Of course she delighted in the filling up
of his woods, she so accustomed to emptiness,
to being taken at face value.
This face, her face eternally the brown
of declining autumn, watches snow inter the grass,
cling to bark making it seem indecisive
about race preference, a fast-to-melt idealism.
With the grass covered, black and white are the only options,
polarity is the only reality; corners aren't neutral
but are on edge.
She shakes off snow, defiance wasted
on the limited audience of horse.
The snow does not hypnotize her as it wants to,
as the blond sun does in making too many prefer daylight.
She has promises to keep,
the promise that she bear Jim no bastards,
the promise that she ride the horse only as long
as it is willing to accept riders,
the promise that she bear Jim no bastards,
the promise to her face that it not be mistaken as shadow,
and miles to go, more than the distance from Africa to Andover,
more than the distance from black to white
before she sleeps with Jim.

NOVEMBER AND AUNT JEMIMA

We sit at the table and that is grace,
the way one commits the prelude to kowtowing
by folding into the chair.

Usually we eat as if on a subway,
among strangers, standing to avoid the
toilet seat. Today, though, is Thanksgiving

so guilt bibs us, an extra place
is set for Aunt Jemima, the pancake box
occupies the chair, the family resemblance

unmistakable. Hips full as Southern Baptist
tents but of a different doctrine.
Teeth white as the shock of lynching, thirty-two

tombstones. Despite the headrag
neither she nor her sister that bore me
are mistaken for gypsies.

The color of corrosion, she is not called
classic. The syrup that is the liquid
version of her skin flows like the promised

milk and honey so once a year we welcome
her. Even Christ would not be welcome every
day. Especially Christ who cannot come

without judgment just as she cannot come
without pancakes, flat, humane stones
still thrown at her by those whose sins

being white are invisible as her pain, the
mix in the box after the grinding of bones.

A RECONSIDERATION
OF THE BLACKBIRD

Let's call him *Jim Crow.*

Let's call him *Nigger* and see if he rises
faster than when we say *abracadabra.*

Guess who's coming to dinner?
Score ten points if you said blackbird.
Score twenty points if you were more specific, as in the first
　　line.

What do you find *from here to eternity?*
Blackbirds.

Who never sang for my father?
The blackbirds who came, one after the other,
landed on the roof
and pressed it down, burying us alive.
Why didn't we jump out the windows? Didn't we
have enough time?
We were outnumbered
(13 on the clothesline, 4 & 20 in the pie).
We were holding hands and hugging like never before.
You could say the blackbirds did us a favor.

Let's not say that however. Instead let the crows speak.
Let them use their tongues or forfeit them.

Problem: What would we do with 13 little black tongues?

Solution: Give them away. Hold them for ransom. Make belts.
Little nooses for little necks.

Problem: The little nooses fit only fingers.

Solution: Get married.

Problem: No one's in love with the blackbirds.

Solution: Paint them white, call them visions, everyone will
want one.

TRIBUTE TO JESSE AND
THEN SOME

Sometimes the only dignity is in walking the streets
in Goodwill shoes that once upon a time transported
other feet to club dates and charity luncheons
where the future is at the discretion of stock brokers
who treat the crystal ball, fragile as the world,
like a piñata at a Mexican theme benefit. They say
olé and *salud* when they toast. The light, dim

as their idea of poverty is yellower, antique
when the vintage alcohol glazes the blood coursing
like liquid rats. This is called a buzz. This
is likened to the charitable work of bees, pollen
pushing, a powder fine as dream sugar, that soft
palette of heroin or innocent double, Block Drug
Company's BC powders folded into waxed paper sleeves
and so suspicious you're better off feeling the neuralgia,
keeping sciatica's ache.

Welfare is about as charitable as America gets
with its limbo stick rules of income to make you
crawl. Then Jesse said it, I heard it with
my own ears, saw it with my own eyes, and now I'm
on my way to tell the king that *Jesus was born homeless*
to a single mother like her counterparts
cloistered in the projects, alleys, subway tunnels,
forsaken buses, tenement nunneries, the order of Mary,
all of them with God-solicited child again and again,
our father still art in heaven so he can't pay child
support but *thy will be done* anyway. One woman

loves her man telepathically; he is gone
until he can find somewhere the work that deserves

pride, that doesn't depend on people spending, using,
wasting, destroying. It was so easy in Hamelin.

Today, there's so many pipers in the neighborhood,
every child is likely to hear the music he can't resist
and groove and hip hop his way into stone, the mausoleum
of a mountain. No more is it comforting

that everyone wants to go home, to the sweet, the humble,
the whorehouse, crackhouse, poorhouse. Do what you
have to, grab some gusto if you can, and if you take stock
in gusto. Otherwise, forget it.

Sometimes scrubbing the rounded front end of the toilet
is like polishing a trophy, a miniature of the winning
yacht. Flush and there's even tides. Steady, steady—
good; the boat doesn't budge, the anchor is mighty, of
brooding iron clenching river bottom dirt that's
being worked on by the water, readied for the making
of men, the hope of all dirt since that first time. And
no, hope is not better than nothing; they're about
the same. But keep it alive anyway, vegetative, attached
to a machine.

REDBONES AS NOTHING SPECIAL

It is 1960 and a crowd is
at Redbones. There is a jukebox, don't
know why I didn't say so before.
The music, the talk, the cuesticks
are all percussion. The rhythm
inculcates that something is stirring
underground, a funky subway.
It can be so dark and dusky in there
teeth, eyes, red lips seem to have come
unescorted. And this is nice.
All the rear ends at Redbones are convex.
This too is nice.

While the good deacons, the fine sisters
boycott W. T. Grant's, they can still
go to Redbones' booths that become pulpits
when the deacons and sisters commence the
laying on of hands. I like the men with
gold teeth, I like to call them paydirt.
The Alabama clay slowdragging
with bicuspids and incisors.

FIVE MIRACLES

1.

We were cutting corn from cobs,
separating pied kernels
into red piles, yellow, black.
We weren't told to do this.
We took it upon ourselves
to make distinctions,
showing off our mother wit:
red into bowls,
yellow into jars with dated labels,
black into the scuttle
by the stove.

2.

Lutie Watson swallowed a snake
when she drank at the creek
that lynchers sank Jo-jo's stone-filled
body in last year;
that snake must have been
his soul transformed
because now she's pregnant again,
way past the age of possibility.

3.

Went to a gypsy.
Gypsy had never seen a lifeline so long.
Stretches from my thumb to my shoulder.

4.

He may be a buck-toothed
ugly dude
but he ain't a sawed-off runt.
Shoulders so broad
looks like his head

sits on a boxcar.
I go walking with him
through them I-talian sections,
them Polish and what-have-you sections,
people damn near bow.
His T-shirt (special made) says:
Home-grown in Darkest Africa.

5.
What's a *nice* colored girl like you
doing in New England?
Thinking about changing my reputation.

A GODIVA

Myself, I always thought it
a throwback revealing primate roots
I'd as soon forget. Oh but what

would I do without that stuff
softer than a hand, a spool
unwound on my head and gold
already, before

the weaver comes with that talent
I share; my one-word name
rivals the best of them:
Rumplestiltskin, God.

My calling came and I went public as
a hedge on horseback in Coventry, the
sun fermenting the color of my hair
into grog that will not

lay wasted. *Eat, drink, be merry,*
those aren't nude words. I put it all
on the table for surgery, not feast.
I want to be cut through to my

black woman's heart. She had one
in 1057 as well as a continent
that had not been reconciled nor
clothed. Breasts hanging as fruit

should, unpicked sculpture on a
tree, museum pieces. She is
something good for you that is not
medicine. And I

am her transmitted, no longer
literal, needful of reasons
to take off clothes that don't explain
living, and distort everything God

gave us, while trying to be
metaphors for the gifts. If I succeed
there is a tax that will die. I ride
like a morbid Midas, my lips

and fingers coax their love objects
into the most golden silence of them all.
The usual death rider got time off
for good behavior. I just worry

that I might like this, that I'll take
my heart out of the black woman and
put it in a dead thing.

FROM THE BRIDE'S JOURNAL

1.

The room fills, refills
without emptying. The light
is dusty and old. His will
holds the wood together, thoughts
compress logs into planks.
Cracks aren't wide enough
for whispers. Cobwebs hang
like pontoon bridges
from one wall to the next.

2.

There's something of a coast
in his profile,
some poached country
where winds knock down trees
and undress them.

3.

The old DeSoto won't start.
I stare through the windshield.
We don't really resemble
the couple in the brochure
as my family suggested.

4.

In the cabin
I sit across from him
keeping on my hat, coat.
He says nothing,
removes my full plate from the table,
takes it outdoors, throws it,
shoots it.

He cracks his knuckles
in the doorway, shakes off snow,
carries me over his shoulder.
His zipper sounds like a saw.

DENIAL

This is supposed to be a denial. The Millers say I stole their toddler. The wife adds that precious wasn't even weaned. I'm supposed to say I never saw the child and that the only Miller I know is beer. I'm supposed to slap my thigh, act like a jolly lesbian who would, if she thought about stealing a toddler, give more consideration to gender. These Millers have a hyperactive boy. I'm told. I'm supposed to say I only resemble the Salvation Army general who rescues kids from abusive and burning homes. I have one of those faces that keeps turning up in newspapers, the police artist's composite sketch. I'm supposed to guffaw at irregular intervals. I'm supposed to hoist my feet on top of the desk and create a sensation by being crass and crude. On the advice of my lawyer I'm not supposed to plead insanity just demonstrate it.

The truth is I kept the baby while they vacationed. The truth is I won their child as payment for their poker debts. The truth is I'm the surrogate and I decided to keep the child. The truth is I had the child. Look at the womb print. I had the child but I lost it. The truth is I'm hooked up to this machine—lie detector, kidney dialysis, cathode ray decoder, automatic D & C and waxer, trying to get the nurse to overdose my morphine. Trying.

ST. ALEXIS HOSPITAL:
VISITING HOUR

I ask if she remembers
when she thought nuns never died.
I haven't seen a dead one yet,
she replies.

From under the bed she pulls out
a trunk full of rosaries.
End to end, they cover a mile.

Then off comes the heavy black skirt
and I tuck her in,
shake crumbs from her missal,
turn off the lamp, let the same
darkness touch us.

She tells me about the crazy nun
who wanted to grow wings,
that every night she massaged
her back with lilies' dew
and Mary's milk.

They can't get her temperature
down.

A CHILD'S BEEN DEAD A WEEK

We take turns
dressing her, propping her
by the window facing the street.
Our miracle is so simple:
a fresh-laid egg—still warm,
cradled against a cheek
then boiled in vinegar—
is opened a little,
taken to an anthill
and buried.
When the egg is consumed
completely, she revives.

We're not welcome in the church.
I get as far as the vestibule,
can even hear the hymns.
An usher opens the door for me.
We need only a *simple* prayer:
Lord, make the ants eat.

THE HARRIDAN

The harridan loses her temper all the time, claims drunk men
looking for a brothel took it; her diary

is full of lies. Two days later
she fishes her temper from the sewer where she lost it.

She grinds it with her teeth, the bitter taste
is sobering until her temper slips through the gaps,

comes out of salt & pepper shakers or the showerhead
and explodes over her like insecticide.

Such losses are minor,
her humpback is a cache. She can go for months

without an oasis, she has gone a whole life.
She does not know what to call this place

where butter clogs the pores of her bread
and suffocates it,

where geese fly backwards
closing their vee like a zipper,

where she has no way of knowing how long
before her upper and lower teeth lock

in her only marriage.

LANDSCAPE WITH SAXOPHONIST

The usual is there,
nondescript trees opened like umbrellas,
pessimists always expecting rain,
chickadees whose folding and unfolding wings
suggest the shuffling and reshuffling
of the cardsharp's deck;
nothing noteworthy except the beginning saxophonist
blowing with the efficacy of wolves addicted to pigs,
blowing down those poorly built houses,
the leaves off the trees, the water in
another direction, the ace of spades
into the ground with the cardsharp's bad intentions.
The discord and stridency set off landslides
and avalanches; his playing moves the earth,
not lovers who are satisfied too quickly
and by the wrong things.

SCENE FROM

THE SPIRIT OF THE BEEHIVE,

A SPANISH FILM

Isabel plays dead for Ana who doesn't mind.
She talks to Isabel, tells her what the dead
still need to know. Isabel just wanted to lie down
with the newly arrived womanhood and she sucks
off the blood lipstick when Ana forsakes the body
to study grass that is brown as a whip not just through
the window. Nothing makes Isabel speak so Ana calls
for *Milagros* the cat, just before a garden glove
covers Ana's face so the molesting can proceed
without sound effects, but it turns out to be Isabel
suddenly upright and scolding her naughty hand
before she runs through and through fire, painting her hair.
That night, Ana goes out, watches the moon rise
as high as anything she has seen ascend.
Her own eyes of blue moon posted in white sky close
and a train bursts through the white smoke
of a clean fire, and the grinding metal relaxes,
the engine tamed.
The daylight is so broad it is exhausting,
shadows too few and minor. A man jumps off the train
into the cloud and the camera prolongs the two or three seconds
in which he flies. Shift to the next morning; the stirrings
are all to subtle, "still" and "calm" yet must be used.
Ana's awakening is a return to her bed opposite the bed
in which Isabel's revival is too sustained to be the miracle.
Ostensibly, Ana dreams but closes her eyes to award herself
privacy, and the man who jumped off the train assumes,
in the abandoned house where Ana has gone
to be the one girl Frankenstein's monster will not kill
and toss like a leaden flower into a lake, he assumes Ana's

position without copying her repose. His is a dirt bed.
The man is supposed to be a criminal but his only
filmed acts have been getting off a train and
seeking shelter; now he pulls out the pocketwatch
of Ana's father and it plays Ana's childhood, a tune
only his eyes follow to envy, and even that he will lose.
This could be the crime, except that Ana gave him the watch
and her father's overcoat where the watch was.
Then it doesn't matter. Then it is another day,
one that brings Ana to the abandoned house's well
whose deepness, echo, chill, and dark hoard complexity
and texture the village needs. The man is gone but Ana
doesn't miss him long, calling almost immediately
upon the monstrous instead of a holy spirit,
extending to it her flower of a hand that will last
for the shortest season. She is singing, but this
I cannot prove.

SPRING CLEANING AT THE
LEWISTON POLICE STATION

In the basement,
a box of human bones
dug up
near the Camas Prairie Railroad Bridge
by accident.
The police were just
doing their job
when they put the bones
in a box
in the basement
and forgot them
for nine years.
A preliminary report in 1971
indicated the bones
may have belonged
to an Indian woman.
No definite opinion
could be obtained
since the bones
couldn't speak.
The University of Idaho
has them now.
If the bones
are Indian bones,
they'll go to the Nez Perce tribe;
if they are not,
they'll go back in the box.

THE NATURE OF MORNING

With arm at the angle for low salute
each tooth is brushed, up and down; my next duty
is raising the flag, full vs. half staff, I can
never decide if there is reason not to mourn.
Forks of sunlight come down as from a farmer stuffing
clouds into his blue silo trying not to sink in it,
trying not to go under, but it's so clear, so
uncomplicated, easier to make sense of than
foreclosure in which he'll drown anyway.
A rake of rays untangles grasses, separates as

in hugs having to end, trains having to pull away,
these things whose attraction is in sameness, their
coalition contrary to the governing magnetism. *Amandla.*

Teeth should sparkle and gleam, not yellow into
brittle pages, obsolescence of the saved first soft-
sided shoe, saved pacifier never in peril. The
yellowed wedding dress, its shoulders padded, skirt
petticoated so that an actual bride is unnecessary.

Here's a reason to mourn: letting the best man get
away, marrying a lesser, nonsuperlative groom.
It happens at every wedding.

Apology travels incognito, in the form of toothbrush,
in the form of maid, doing my dirty work for me, keeping
my hands clean, my elbows off the table, my mind
off the farmer. This much is right: Grace
must precede the meal, for teeth are gladiators.

THE WRECKAGE ON THE
WALL OF EGGS

I cried over Humpty-Dumpty.
My indulgent parents permitted mock funerals
after every breakfast. The wall is what upset me,
Humpty's segregation which I doubt he chose.
The King's obligatory visit to the site of disaster.
I cried eggs then double dutched through shells.
One summer I logged a hundred miles in the driveway.
I was after the King's men and had no hope of catching them
since I lived on the wall. Total unobstructed vision
and I loathed it. On both sides were hundreds of girls
perfect for the part of Heidi.
My jump rope flew like long braids I didn't have.
The granite street was a long tombstone for my grandfathers
and their fathers. Following it would not lead to Dörfli
in the Alps. The easiest thing was to keep looking east and west
and hating girls who couldn't control ancestry.
On the wall, all we ever want is easiness.
Eggshells keep turning up on the path, the humpty-dumpties
spill from me and die like so many babies mercy-killed
out of slavery.
My life on the wall is anything but easy.
I want to but can't hate Heidi well.
I can't maintain tragic responses to breaking eggs.
When I look down at the wreckage on the wall of eggs that
came out of me, I see that what's inside is as white and
gold as Heidi.

SUNRISE COMES TO
SECOND AVENUE

Daylight announces
the start of a day six hours old.

We all have thankless
jobs to do. Consider

the devotion of fishes singing
hymns without voices.

The clock's hands searching
for the lost face, a place

for the Eucharist. The man
bedded down on the roadway,

the asphalt pope out of bread,
breath and blessings.

The streetcleaner
sweeping up confessions.

AFTERNOON NAP

Ansted fits both ways in his crib
and whispers as he catalogs sleep

turning everything delicate; every
hissy sound becomes praise and

everything makes it; the diesel-fed
hulks shod with eighteen round shoes

convert to tiptoe according to what
distance filters. The gurgling

steam pipes become discreet, conduct
their affairs in the basement and

make just warmth public. One week
when the heat should not have been off

we trembled, family of four, and were
turned, scale magnification of the give

in the strings of a treble instrument
in the right hands.

AN ANOINTING

Boys have to slash their fingers to become brothers. Girls trade their Kotex, me and Molly do in the mall's public facility.

Me and Molly never remember each other's birthdays. On purpose. We don't like scores of any kind. We don't wear watches or weigh ourselves.

Me and Molly have tasted beer. We drank our shampoo. We went to the doctor together and lifted our specimen cups in a toast. We didn't drink that stuff. We just gargled.

When me and Molly get the urge, we are careful to put it back exactly as we found it. It looks untouched.

Between the two of us, me and Molly have 20/20 vision.

Me and Molly are in eighth grade for good. We like it there. We adore the view. We looked both ways and decided not to cross the street. Others who'd been to the other side didn't return. It was a trap.

Me and Molly don't double date. We don't multiply anything. We don't know our multiplication tables from a coffee table. We'll never be decent waitresses, indecent ones maybe.

Me and Molly do not believe in going ape or going bananas or going Dutch. We go as who we are. We go as what we are.

Me and Molly have wiped each other's asses with ferns. Made emergency tampons of our fingers. Me and Molly made do with what we have.

Me and Molly are in love with wiping the blackboard with each other's hair. The chalk gives me and Molly an idea of what old age is like; it is dusty and makes us sneeze. We are allergic to it.

Me and Molly, that's M and M, melt in your mouth.

What are we doing in your mouth? Me and Molly bet you'll never guess. Not in a million years. We plan to be around that long. Together that long. Even if we must freeze the moment and treat the photograph like the real thing.

Me and Molly don't care what people think. We're just glad that they do.

Me and Molly lick the dew off the morning grasses but taste no honey till we lick each other's tongues.

We wear full maternity sails. We boat upon my broken water. The katabatic action begins, Molly down my canal binnacle first, her water breaking in me like an anointing.

THE RAPTURE OF DRY ICE
BURNING OFF SKIN AS THE
MOMENT OF THE SOUL'S
APOTHEOSIS

How will we get used to joy
if we won't hold onto it?

Not even extinction stops me; when
I've sufficient craving, I follow the buffalo,
their hair hanging below their stomachs like
fringes on Tiffany lampshades; they can be turned on
so can I by a stampede, footsteps whose sound
is my heart souped up, doctored, ninety pounds
running off a semi's invincible engine. Buffalo
heaven is Niagara Falls. There their spirit
gushes. There they still stampede and power
the generators that operate the Tiffany lamps
that let us see in some of the dark. Snow
inundates the city bearing their name; buffalo
spirit chips later melt to feed the underground,
the politically dredlocked tendrils of roots. And this
has no place in reality, is trivial juxtaposed with

the faces of addicts, their eyes practically as sunken
as extinction, gray ripples like hurdlers' track lanes
under them, pupils like just more needle sites.
And their arms: flesh trying for a moon apprenticeship,
a celestial antibody. Every time I use it
the umbrella is turned inside out,
metal veins, totally hardened arteries and survival
without anything flowing within, nothing saying
life came from the sea, from anywhere but coincidence

or God's ulcer, revealed. Yet also, inside out
the umbrella tries to be a bouquet, or at least
the rugged wrapping for one that must endure much,
without dispensing coherent parcels of scent,
before the refuge of vase in a room already accustomed
to withering mind and retreating skin. But the smell
of the flowers lifts the corners of the mouth as if
the man at the center of this remorse has lifted her
in a waltz. This is as true as sickness. The Jehovah's

Witness will come to my door any minute with tracts, an
inflexible agenda and I won't let him in because
I'm painting a rosy picture with only blue and
yellow (sadness and cowardice).
I'm something of an alchemist. Extinct.
He would tell me time is running out.
I would correct him: time *ran* out; that's why
history repeats itself, why we can't advance.
What joy will come has to be here right now: Cheer
to wash the dirt away, Twenty Mule Team Borax and
Arm & Hammer to magnify Cheer's power, lemon-scented
bleach and ammonia to trick the nose, improved—changed—
Tide, almost all-purpose starch that cures any limpness
except impotence. Celebrate that there's *Master*card
to rule us, bring us to our knees, the protocol we follow
in the presence of the head of our state of ruin, the
official with us all the time, not inaccessible in
palaces or White Houses or Kremlins. Besides every
ritual is stylized, has patterns and repetitions
suitable for adaptation to dance. Here come toe shoes,
brushstrokes, oxymorons. Joy

is at our tongue tips: Let the great thirsts and hungers
of the world be the *marvelous* thirsts, *glorious* hungers.
Let heartbreak be alternative to coffeebreak, five
midmorning minutes devoted to emotion.

MAI PEN RAI

I listen to the ragman's throaty drawl
as the curtains blow over me like mosquito netting.
His voice reminds me of chanting women doing laundry
with stones. Their hair falls over their eyes
like a curtain in shreds.
One of the Thai women pulls from the water a limb
washed down from Laos that doesn't match yesterday's.
She wears gifts from the ragman
who is now just below my window.
His stake-body truck moves as slow as a glacier.
The Thai woman can't move at all, the limbs are all around her,
a bone fence two feet high and growing.
At our family reunion we suck spareribs, purging them
of meat and marrow before we toss them.
They are not at all like boomerangs. The Thai woman
keeps these gifts too; it is warm inside the pyramid of bone.
I wish the ragman would wipe his forehead and unbutton
his shirt. I wish he wanted lemonade
and a date with the Thai woman.
Her arms can hold all the empty cradles in the Holy Land.
Her arms make whatever they contain holy.
A grenade in her arms is a bad egg
yet she sits on it and waves away observers, bids them run.
On behalf of stunted Bolivian Indians, shadows
pursued across the veldt and crippled one-legged crosses,
she lifts the sky saying *Mai pen rai, mai pen rai,
it doesn't matter.*
Perhaps I'd prefer mimosas, strawberries in season
and the view from Pike's Peak but not in this life;
everyday the ragman's drawl says *mai pen rai, mai pen rai*
and I believe.

A CATCHER FOR AN ATOMIC BOUQUET

I have just watched "Eyes on the Prize"
twenty years after the contest. I am looking
at my winnings: a husband who is not literary,
a baby from a teenager's body, a daughter
from a sister-in-law declared unfit, who is
legally daughter no more, barely even niece
she has so estranged herself from the meaning
of family, carrying but for the grace of God
the child of her biological father;
and the grand prize: my own biological baby at last
and the end of excuses. Stop. This maze
is not the prize. Stop. Writers, so many
believe, must write about what they know
instead of what they want to know.

I have played that game to toss a quarter
into a milk bottle with a hymen. I left
the kiosk, stuffed flamingos and Saint Bernards
still suspended from the ceiling
like plucked chickens, ducks, onions, eels
at a Hangzhou outdoor market.

They are practically immutable fixtures.
That is the way luck would have it and luck
officiates in any matter of prize
no matter how effectively the loser
insists on fairness; it is infertile insistence
yet sometimes that is the prize, what is not
brought into the world.

For consolation
there's always the faces of Hiroshima

that stayed on the walls, apocalyptic posters.
Apocalyptic rewards.
No one caught the bouquet thrown
at the nuclear wedding. Exploding flowers
as from a joke shop.

Right now I've got my eye on the flamingo
withdrawing at least one leg he insists
won't be shit on.

GOODNESS AND THE SALT
OF THE EARTH

Somebody's husband raped you while you were supposed to be in the choir pounding a tambourine, not a chest. Early Sunday morning, must have been an Easter Sunday because something came back from death; it came with a wedding ring and it was black and it smiled and it was good. You got pregnant. Good. Had an abortion. Good. That's what the Lord said in Genesis; he saw the world and what was happening, and it was still good. So you were good and turned the pages, read every line, and Lot's wife, that good woman, turned to salt because she was polite and couldn't leave without saying good-bye. You said it in the hospital: "Good-bye, Baby, you never cried, just ate salt and died, just got tossed over the left shoulder. You broke. I never got a chance to see myself in you." In church the sisters shouted, fainted. O hallelujah! O the glory! Ushers came running, *smell the salt, Sister; smell the salt.* Sometimes it brings you back. Sometimes it kills. Don't trust it. Stay away from bacon, ham, all cured meat. Stay away from uncles licking palms so the salt sticks. Stay away from men. Stay away from angry crowds yelling, "Salt, Peter. Salt, Peter." Ask the saint for something else. It always rains. It always pours. Thank goodness.

ALMOST AN ODE TO THE WEST
INDIAN MANATEE

When James Balog said *her snout was soft as deerskin*
but the rest of her hide had the rough tautness of a football
made of sandpaper, that was ode enough.

In the facing photo, the hamadryas baboon snubs me, her
nose's uptilt such that the nostrils are mosques
dark with shed sins and the doom that opposes pilgrimage.
She is in love.

I'll buy that; what can't happen at a Florida circus
with twin monkey girls (their hair like pipeworks follows
the spines beneath their costumes exiting mid-rump slits like
prehensile tails neglected into dredlock rip-off) and a resident
hawker whose chest hair grows in question marks? Also

Guernsey cow with six stomachs each separately fed by the
angle of head at grazing, the particulars of the lowing, variety
of the moo, the sweetness of the quackgrass and clover
and all the different mood-matched milks on country tables
in pitchers with pouring lips wide as a pelvic bone.

The rhino's horn hollowed out is cornucopian. I never
think of this when it would do some good. Already
the manatee and baboon are starting to taste extinction,
welcoming it as resolution of a forgotten craving deep in
the proliferation of Guernsey cream white as a light-emitting
lake that makes manatee and baboon glow when they catch sight
of themselves during their dive at the moment in which
the dive becomes inevitable, the cream displacing
into a crown as they enter, then settling
as if they never existed.

THERE WILL BE ANIMALS

There will be animals to teach us
what we can't teach ourselves.

There will be a baboon who is neither stupid nor clumsy
as he paints his mandrill face for the war being waged
against his jungle.

There will be egrets in a few thousand years
who will have evolved without plumes so we cannot take them.

There will be ewes giving and giving their wool
compensating for what we lack in humility.

There will be macaws with short arched bills
that stay short because they talk without telling lies.

Mackerel will continue to appear near Cape Hatteras each spring
and swim north into Canadian waters so there can be continuity.

There will be penguins keeping alive Hollywood's golden era.

The chaparral cock will continue to outdistance man
twisting and turning on a path unconcerned with shortcuts.

Coffin fly dun will leave the Shawsheen River
heading for the lights of Lawrence. What they see in 48 hours
makes them adults who will fast for the rest of their short lives,
mating once during the next hour and understanding everything
as they drop into a communal grave three feet thick with family
reaching the same conclusions.

The coast horned lizard still won't be found
without a bag of tricks; it will inflate and the first

of six million Jewfish will emerge from its mouth.
We will all be richer.

John Dory will replace John Doe
so the nameless among us will have Peter's thumbmark
on their cheek
and the coin the saint pulled from their mouths
in their pockets. Then once and for all
we will know it is no illusion:
The lion lying with the lamb, the grandmother
and Little Red Riding Hood
walking out of a wolf named Dachau.

MISS LIBERTY LOSES PAGEANT

Should be a headline but it's not
newsworthy, more ordinary than anchovies
gossiping olfactions of fishy scandal.

The Lady of the Harbor, Fatima rip-off
except she came first with a crown like
the one of thorns on another whose cause is

masses. Avant-garde refugee from 50's horror
flick *Attack of the 50-foot Woman,* here turned
to stone fleeing Gomorrah, Gotham, some G (god-

damned) place. *There she is, Miss America, your
ideal;* there must be a mistake, Miss Liberty
should have won. Why was there a contest? And

what about that talent? Professional model, posed,
picture perfect. Mannequin displayed where the world
window shops. In case of emergency, break glass.

She lost her fire. Holds an ice-cream cone.
Maybe she'll court Prometheus, this green old
paradoxical maid in Spinster Army uniform.

Basic Training long over, revolutions too
yet she earned no stars or stripes, no rank,
not even private; she's public, communal,

free. How happy she must be, every day
at the beach, keeping to the shallows, barely
up to her knees. No lifeguard is on duty.

Her back is to us while she changes
her mind about walking away, entering
the deep seat of meaning she thought furnished

her house. She sits at the water table,
a feast has been laid for Squanto or Hobbamock
and she is it. They will be converts. Guests

not hosts. A hot night in July, fireworks
popping instead of corn. These are new ways
of business as usual. The struggle to be taken

seriously prevails over the better instinct of
not being taken at all. She is in moonlight,
her toes loosen caviar; if the sun gets the angle

right, it will sink in her torch and proxy a candle.
How romantic is the notion. Better that she gets
the man than Dudley Do-Right whose name is plea.

GREEN LIGHT AND
GAMMA WAYS

Miss Liberty is green, the horizon and sky
plus yellow skin.
She is a minority too,
color of ridiculous Martian fable
and not a man.
Handicapped, disabled.
Another immigrant.

Green light is not like the Pacific.
Green light is not like jade.
You can see it when money changes,
transforms hands;
green light is the power to go for it.
It is shined on Miss Liberty,
has no inner genesis.
But it warms her.

ONE FOR ALL NEWBORNS

They kick and flail like crabs on their backs.
Parents outside the nursery window do not believe
they might raise assassins or thieves, at the very worst
a poet or obscure jazz musician whose politics
spill loudly from his horn.
Everything about it was wonderful, the method
of conception, the gestation, the womb opening
in perfect analogy to the mind's expansion.
Then the dark succession of constricting years,
mother competing with daughter for beauty and losing,
varicose veins and hot-water bottles, joy boiled away,
the arrival of knowledge that eyes are birds with clipped wings,
the sun at a 30° angle and unable to go higher, parents
who cannot push anymore, who stay by the window
looking for signs of spring
and the less familiar gait of grown progeny.
I am now at the age where I must begin to pay
for the way I treated my mother. My daughter is just like me.
The long trip home is further delayed, my presence
keeps the plane on the ground. If I get off, it will fly.
The propeller is a cross spinning like a buzz saw
about to cut through me. I am haunted and my mother is not
      dead.
The miracle was not birth but that I lived despite my crimes.
I treated God badly also; he is another parent
watching his kids through a window, eager to be proud
of his creation, looking for signs of spring.

ACKNOWLEDGMENTS

The following poems, many in different versions, appeared originally in books by Thylias Moss. From *Hosiery Seams on a Bowlegged Woman*, Cleveland State University Press, 1983: "Alternatives for a Celibate Daughter," "Life in a Sterile Environment: A Case Study" (retitled: "The Manna Addicts"), "Rush Hour," "One-legged Cook," "The Day Before Kindergarten: Taluca, Alabama, 1959," "Five Miracles," "From the Bride's Journal," "Denial," "St. Alexis Hospital: Visiting Hour," "A Child's Been Dead a Week," "Spring Cleaning at the Lewiston Police Station," "Goodness and the Salt of the Earth," and "Old Maids Weaving Baskets." From *Pyramid of Bone*, The University Press of Virginia, 1990: "Fisher Street," "The Owl in Daytime," "The Undertaker's Daughter Makes Bread," "The Undertaker's Daughter Feels Neglect," "Passover Poem," "Doubts During Catastrophe," "Running Out of Choices," *"Timex* Remembered," "A Reconsideration of the Blackbird," "The Harridan," "Landscape with Saxophonist," "The Wreckage on the Wall of Eggs," *"Mai Pen Rai,"* "There Will Be Animals," and "One for All Newborns." From *At Redbones*, Cleveland State University Press, 1990: "Washing Bread," "Fullness," "The Adversary," "The Eclipse and the Holy Man," "Raising a Humid Flag," "For Those Who Can't Peel the Potatoes Close Enough," "Spilled Sugar," "The Party to Which Wolves Are Invited," "Death of the Sweet World," "The Eyelid's Struggle," "She Did My Hair Outside, the Wash a Tent Around Us," "She's Florida Missouri but She Was Born in Valhermosa and Lives in Ohio," "To Buckwheat and Other Pickaninnies" (retitled: "A Little Something for Buckwheat and Other Pickaninnies"), "Lunchcounter Freedom," "The Root of the Road," "November and Aunt Jemima," "Redbones as Nothing Special," "A Godiva," "Sunrise Comes to Second Avenue," and "A Catcher for an Atomic Bouquet." From *Rainbow Remnants in Rock Bottom Ghetto Sky*, Persea Books, 1991: "All Is Not Lost When Dreams Are," "The Warmth of Hot Chocolate," "Poem for My Mothers and Other Makers of Asafetida," "The Linoleum Rhumba," "Birmingham Brown's Turn," "The Lynching," "Interpretation of a Poem by Frost," "The Nature of Morning," *"An Anointing,"* "The Rapture of Dry Ice Burning Off Skin as the Moment of the Soul's Apotheosis," "Almost an Ode to the West Indian Manatee," "Miss Liberty Loses Pageant," "What Hung Above Our Heads Like Truce" (retitled: "One-eyed Mother, Selling Mangoes"), "Congregations" (retitled: "Small Congregations"), "Detour: The Death of

Agnes" (retitled: "The Wonder"), and "Green Light and Gamma Ways." Some poems not previously published in book form have appeared in the following publications: *Antæus, Callaloo, Colorado Review, The New York Times, Onthebus, Red Brick Review,* and *River Styx.*